Messages from Thomas
Raising Psychic Children

Also by James F. Twyman
(all available from Findhorn Press)

Emissary of Light: A Vision of Peace[1]

Emissary of Love: The Psychic Children Speak to the World[2]

The Secret of the Beloved Disciple

Portrait of the Master

The Prayer of St. Francis

Praying Peace

The Praying Peace Cards

Ten Spiritual Lessons I Learned at the Mall

1. Available from Warner Books in the USA/Canada

2. Available from Hampton Roads outside UK and Europe

Messages from Thomas
Raising Psychic Children

James F. Twyman

First published by Findhorn Press 2003

ISBN 1 84409 014 0

British Library Cataloguing-in-Publication Data.
A catalogue record for this book is available from the British Library.

Edited by Shari Mueller
Cover and interior design: Thierry Bogliolo
Cover photo © Thinkstock
Printed and bound by WS Bookwell, Finland

Published by
Findhorn Press
305a The Park, Findhorn
Forres IV36 3TE
Scotland, UK
tel 01309 690582
fax 01309 690036
e-mail: info@findhornpress.com
findhornpress.com

Contents

About James F. Twyman

James is an internationally renowned author and musician who travels the world performing "The Peace Concert" in some of the greatest areas of violence and discord. Also known as the "Peace Troubadour," he has been invited by government officials and humanitarian organizations to perform in countries like Iraq, Northern Ireland, Bosnia, Serbia, Kosovo, Israel, East Timor, and Mexico, as well as the United Nations in New York. He blends his unique style of music with his international reputation for drawing millions of people together in prayer to influence the process of peace in countries torn apart by hatred and war.

His ministry began in 1994, when he took the peace prayers from the twelve major religions of the world and arranged them to music. His goal was to demonstrate that all spiritual paths point to a single expression: Peace. Since 1995, James has helped sponsor several major prayer vigils that have been attended by millions around the world.

James Twyman is also the founder of the "Cloth of Many Colors" peace project, which weaves the prayers of hundreds of thousands of people from around the world into a single quilt nearly a mile long. This amazing quilt was presented at the United Nations in New York, the Pentagon in Washington, and was literally wrapped around the U.S. Capitol on September 20, 2000.

For more information on retreats and programs with James Twyman, visit his website at >www.JamesTwyman.com<.

INTRODUCTION

I first met Thomas in May of 2001 when I was visiting a remote monastery in the mountains of Bulgaria. At first glance, he seemed like a normal, inquisitive ten-year-old boy, but I soon learned that none of the children I saw at the monastery met my definition of ordinary. Four children were living with the monks at that time, two boys and two girls. They were brought there by their parents because it was the best place in Bulgaria for psychic children to hone their skills, or to learn how to use the real power behind their psychic gifts ... Love! This was what the monks focused on in their training. They taught the children that love is the only true motivation in the universe, and that it is the foundation and essence of every living being. Psychic powers mean nothing without it, for without love they have no heart. This is, the monks taught, what life is all about: Finding our Heart and Living Peace. Properly directed, these children would someday guide the world into this profound realization. The children are the final link to creating a world of compassion and peace.

In the book, *Emissary of Love: the Psychic Children Speak to the World,* I chronicled the amazing journey that led me to the psychic children's school in the Bulgarian mountains. (It has no name, as far as I know, only the name of the monastery, which is a well-kept secret.) I thought that when I returned home, the journey had reached a natural conclusion, then I would write the story and go back to my ordinary life. I should have known better. These journeys never really end, just shift and move from one chapter to the next. They are like the verses of a song, tales of spirited adventures in far away lands, but the final stanza never arrives. And neither do we want it to arrive for it means we have come to the end of something within ourselves, something we don't want to face or see. Our imaginations flourish and our dreams explode, all to reveal a life we share and recognize, though for most of us it is still a faint reflection. And so for me the adventure with the psychic children had just begun, and there was no telling where it would lead.

I soon learned that the monastery I found in Bulgaria was not unique. For at least twenty years, educators and scientists (even governments) have realized that today's children are being born with new depths and higher perceptions. We call them "psychic" or "indigo," but they also evade these labels. They are simply you and I with eyes wide open. They come into the world with the shades up and the windows polished clean. They see the world as it really is, not as we have created it, and they are here to promote this vision. They look at the adults in the world and say, "Why can't you see what we see? It is so clear to us." And with this challenge an opportunity is created, the opportunity to open our own eyes and see what is really there. That's when everything changes, first in our lives, then in the world. That's what the new children are here to reveal—and they will succeed.

Countries like Russia, China, and Japan have been observing the psychic children for years. On a recent trip to Japan, I learned that there are over 400 schools in that country helping children open their minds to these unique abilities. At one point in China, every child had to undergo psychic tests in order to identify those with natural talent. The number they found, though classified, is said to be staggering. A program in South Korea called Brain Respiration showed how easily children can be taught these skills. On a number of occasions they took hundreds of ordinary children and led them through a three-day seminar designed to open their minds and hearts. In the first session the children were tested for psychic powers, and the results were normal. Only a few exhibited a low degree of natural talent. On the third day, however, after undergoing a series of fun exercises, they were tested again. As many as 60% of the children were able to do things like read words written on cards that were sealed inside thick envelopes, or recognize colors that were projected from the mind of another person. This was not a phenomenon that was reserved for a limited number of exceptional children, but something that could be accessed by nearly two-thirds of that group.

The children have a message for the adults of the world—all of us—and they say it is crucial that we learn it now. They believe that the human race stands at a crossroads ... are we on the brink of a new evolution of consciousness, or a continuing spiral leading to fear and war? The sides are being drawn and each one of us must choose where we stand. Their words echo ancient prophesies from many aboriginal cultures, most of which have stories of what to look for during this time some of them call "The Great Shift." Many if not most of those stories are coming true today. The lesson is simple: We have the power to create either a world of peace and compassion—or a world of conflict and war. We have always had this choice, but now it is critical.

This was the basic message Thomas brought to me. Each of the children I met in Bulgaria had a special skill. Thomas' skill was sending thoughts to others. I experienced this gift when I was with him physically, but I had no idea he could do the same over long distances. I was home in Ashland, Oregon in January 2002, soaking in a hot tub in the back yard when I had a strange sense that someone was watching me, and I turned to see if it was true. I didn't see or hear anyone, but the feeling persisted. Then I felt his presence—Thomas—just as I felt it when I saw him last. But that was impossible, I thought to myself. He was thousands of miles away, probably not even at the monastery anymore. Yet I was sure I felt him, and I couldn't shake the strange yet wonderful feeling.

Then thoughts began flooding into my brain, thoughts I knew were not my own. They were Thomas' thoughts, and at first they didn't make any sense at all. I felt like a computer with a program being downloaded into it, but I couldn't open the program to see what it meant, what he intended for me to understand. I jumped out of the hot tub and ran to the computer in my office. I placed my fingers near the keys and hoped something would happen, anything that wouldn't seem too strange. At first there was only silence in the room, but then something changed. I felt my fingers begin to move and the ideas became concrete. I wrote down the first message from Thomas, which was clearly meant for the whole world.

Two other messages followed, and by the time I was through typing I knew something was happening I couldn't explain. However, it was possible nothing was happening at all, that it was just my imagination playing tricks on me. It was the most obvious possibility, and my rational mind jumped on it. After all, it happened while I was soaking in a hot tub, when my mind was blurred and steam clouded my judgment. I tend to be powerfully rational, though many would claim the opposite. Books I've written in the past indicate a willingness to believe what the majority of the population considers impossible. But most of these experiences were at least based on real events, things that happened to me when I was awake and which I could reach out and touch. This was definitely of a different order. I wasn't even sure it happened, and yet the power of the messages compelled me to share them.

We sent an e-mail to a few thousand people describing the experience and offering the messages. I figured there would be a large number of people interested, maybe three or four thousand. But within two weeks there were over twenty-six thousand e-mails from around the world asking to receive the Thomas Messages. Word spread as people forwarded the message from one person to the next, and we were inundated with passionate requests. The messages went out and I could still feel a tinge of wonderment. I felt like I had ventured out on the furthest branch from the trunk, and I started to listen for that distinctive cracking sound.

The response could not have been more different. There were days when we received over a thousand e-mails thanking us for the messages from Thomas. It was so hard for me to believe, and yet the evidence was unavoidable. People's lives were being changed, and that was more important than all my questions. Like Jesus once said, "You judge a tree by the fruit that it bears," and this tree was definitely bearing good fruit.

More messages from Thomas followed, and the e-mail list swelled. Soon there were over fifty thousand people receiving regular inspirational messages from a ten-year-old boy in Bulgaria. The idea of going back to the monastery and tracking him down did occur to me, but I knew it wasn't what he wanted. It wasn't about Thomas and it wasn't about me. It was about the wisdom of the children that was coming at us from nearly every direction. As long as we were listening, that's all they really cared about. Time was of the essence, Thomas kept saying, as if time mattered at all.

More and more people were contacting us for advice on raising their own psychic children. One of my assistants, Sharon Williams, accepted the task of shepherding these people and offering the little wisdom we possessed. As for me, other than raising my own daughter who was by then sixteen, I didn't feel I was much of an authority. There were people around the world who had been working with gifted children for many years, and they were the ones to offer the best advice. The idea arose to write a book that would guide people through the joys and pitfalls of raising the new children. I think the idea came from Thomas, though I'm not sure. I called a few friends I knew would be wonderful resources and asked them to contribute an article or a letter. One by one the pieces fell in place, and this book is what emerged.

I went back to the hot tub and hoped Thomas would return. I didn't have to wait long, though I didn't believe his messages would come in the form of brief insights, poetic and profound. They were clearly meant to trigger the right brain, while the articles written by others were focused more on the left brain. Though they didn't follow any logical course, I felt an intelligence that amazed me winding through each insight Thomas offered. This wasn't at all what I expected when I sat down to begin writing. I felt a collaboration taking place between the mind of Thomas—wherever he was—and my own mind. They were his ideas combined with my words. I can't say I was channeling, for that assumes I was being used as a passive vehicle. I was anything but passive. It's impossible to completely explain what happened, especially since I don't know myself, only that we were working together to create something neither one of us could do alone.

You are going to find some incredible wisdom in this book, both from the authors of the many articles, and from Thomas himself. The words he inspired are the threads that bridge the gap, from poetic verses of truth to the realistic advice offered by experts in the field. What Thomas offers comes from a deep reservoir of experience that transcends the conscious intellect—profound insights from all the psychic children—while the articles and letters come from people who are actually doing the work in the world—from authors to parents and grandparents. This book is a rich collection of action and insight, moving between the left and right hemispheres of the brain with equal ease, opening our minds to possibilities we might have never considered otherwise.

There is one primary message that seems to rise from every article and insight in this book. It is so simple, but if we can fully grasp its importance then the art of raising our children to be open to their gifts will come with extraordinary ease. "Your children chose you and you chose them to do profound work on the planet. You are raising each other for this purpose." So as you read these words keep this idea at the front of your mind. It is the beginning and the end, the alpha and the omega. You are both the parent and the child. There is no real difference.

Enjoy!

1.

Do you want to know who we are?
Some of you call us the Indigo Children,
Or the Psychic Children,
Or even the Crystal Children.
None of that makes sense to us.
Even the word Child no longer applies.
We do look like children
And even act as you would expect us to act.
But that is not who we are.

It is the same for you.
You look one way and act another.
But that does not define who you are.
You are still a child,
And your mind exists within ours.
We are all of that,
Just as you are as well.
It is hard to define what has no definition.

But there is one way I can tell you who we are.

2.

We are You!

Be*lieve* . . . Be *Love.*

By Theresa Stuesser

The article you are about to read is less a set of directives and more a new set for the mind (i.e. a new mindset). In fact, it is also less about us raising the psychic children and more about them raising us. We believe the children are coming in at this time to raise our collective vibration and consciousness from a place of fear and doubt back to one of love and belief—love of all that is, and belief that this raising is possible. They want to assure us that to be*lieve* is to be *love.*

This message about believing is a true tale of releasing old paradigms and embracing the new. Our hope is that you will walk away moved, and perhaps changed in a way that guides you to more fully live from your heart, while honoring the children, as well as your own inner child.

As the children call you to read on, *be love,* and also be open to the trip you are about to take. My husband and I have found the journey we call life to be most joyful when we are completely open to the possibilities that life itself offers, even when its offerings seem to lie just beyond belief. Know that life comes fully equipped with blessed suspension—but only if we're open to it, and, only if we are being love in the process. Be love, believe, and be full of joy, for that is how we can best serve the children, and in the process, ourselves.

∞∞∞

Over 100 cities in more than 60 countries participated in this year's worldwide celebration of peace known as *Earthdance.* The motto of this festival, which hosts the world's largest synchronized dance vigil, is "Give Peace a Dance." We were fortunate to have an *Earthdance 2002* festival in our hometown this year, complete with a large grassy area that served as the dance floor. Our family's first experience with this festival was very special as our dear friend, James Twyman, was leading a cyber prayer vigil from Baghdad, Iraq that coincided with the energy of this worldwide event. At 4 p.m., in Ashland, Oregon, hundreds of us gathered in a big circle, hand-in-hand, to connect to one another in prayer. As we collectively sent love and peace around the globe, Shanti, our infant daughter, crawling as if an unseen someone was beckoning her to come forward, led me toward the center of the circle.

Here, inside the circle, I was taken back to the festival my husband Brian and I had put on two weeks prior. The name of our festival was *The First Annual Festival of the Angels: The Year of the Child.* The idea of organizing a festival for children came to me, out of the blue, while meditating in a steamy tub of hot water. Strangely enough, it felt as if a group of children was talking to me mind-to-mind ... sharing their ideas. Our daughter, quite uncharacteristically, had gone to bed before the sun did, so I decided to treat myself to a candle-lit bath. After my bath, I too, went off to dreamland, with this new thought of a children's festival dancing in my head.

The following morning, Brian noticed an email from James, whom we had recently met. Brian shared that it was a "Thomas message" asking everyone to meditate in hot water in order to better connect with the psychic children. Considering the experience of the night before, this was obviously quite profound to me; I felt that that was exactly who had given me the idea for the festival!

Intuitively, I knew that the goal of the festival was to anchor the energy of love from the children in and around Ashland. I didn't really stop to ask: Why our city, and why us? It seemed much too important to worry about such minor details. I knew, deep in my soul, that it was bigger than the two of us—even bigger than our community. I mentally told Spirit that if it were to be, to just bring on the players and the materials and we would make sure it happened.

Much of the inspiration for specific details of the festival came as I was playing with our daughter, Shanti Grace. I mean this in a very literal way. It was as if a bringing in of Spirit (inspiration, if you will) occurred when I was really present for her—like our connection served as a conduit for a Universal Love Force that was happy to guide us to something that was beyond ourselves. The festival did happen; many came, many healed. We began the festivities with a baby blessing to use the pure new energy that these new little beings radiate as a focus. Although the festival centered on children, many adults said *they* were the ones who were transformed! It was as if everyone, regardless of their age, allowed themselves to be a child as they stepped upon the concrete platform that staged the event.

During the festival, love was anchored and then sent spinning around the globe like a giant web. Interestingly enough, James (Jimmy, as we have come to know and love him) was guided to participate in the two-day festival, bringing closure by singing songs of love and peace. Somehow, I felt that our work with him was just beginning. With that thought, I was suddenly brought back to the present by Shanti's laughter and the feeling of peace emanating from the *Earthdance* circle.

As *Earthdance 2002* was drawing to a close (the final band of the night was performing a quick sound check), I felt the strong impulse to go home. I found myself at first suggesting then directing us to head out. Sitting in the back seat on the ride home, I felt an energy come to me that I can only explain as a download of information. As I felt myself open somehow, I received a message that, at the time, I could not put into words. It was far too complex for any language I knew, almost multi-dimensional. Yet, it seemed so simple when I listened with my heart. I knew it was a message of love. Could the experience of participating in the worldwide *Prayer for Peace* have triggered this opening? I wondered.

The following questions then popped into my head, one after another: Is this urgent message of love coming from the psychic children? Is this somehow connected to additional work we'll be doing with Jimmy? Where in the world is this coming from? Perhaps it's coming from Shanti (who was sound asleep next to me in her car seat) I reasoned. Perhaps it was the psychic kids who were responsible for bringing us all together in the first place! Our daughter giggled softly in her sleep.

The possibilities were, and still are, mind-boggling! I felt these little bits of information that I was receiving, even though I was unable to interpret them with specific words, were coming for a reason I was not yet able to comprehend. I mentally sent out the thought, "Wait, hold on. Before you send any more ... what in the world am I supposed to do with all this stuff?" With that thought, I got an answer: *It is to be expressed through some kind of creative project, a "medium" of sorts.* At first, I thought it was to be a painting, or perhaps a sculpture ... maybe even a book. "A book?" I muttered under my breath. I knew that this information had to come through a medium that held the potential to express what I believed to be profound communication of transformational dimension. The message needed the right channel to broadcast its loving frequency, and it was begging for my attention.

Though it took me quite some time to recognize it, I now know part of the message I received that night is found within these pages. Yes, the medium is this article, in part; it is also me. And, it is you, as well. In fact, it is all of us. We are all vehicles, instruments in a sense ... instruments of love.

I believe we are being asked to imagine the following: What if, by reading this article, an intuitive switch is activated, or several small switches perhaps, somewhere deep inside our being. What if this re-circuiting, or attunement if you will, allows us to more clearly tune in to all that is around us, thereby creating an opening—an opening that causes a gradual or instant awakening. Maybe, just maybe it will help us to see what's real ... what's true ... and, what's possible.

What if this change clears our mind chatter and the distractions around us, so that we may more clearly see, hear, sense, and know? What if it dissolves feelings of judgment and anger and transforms them into feelings of compassion and joy? Can something like that be possible? Furthermore, what if the psychic kids in our presence are behind it all, busily guiding us to construct the grid of love that will make it all possible? Is this beyond belief? Imagine if everyone believed that peace was not only a possibility, but was a reality waiting to be realized! What a different world this could be!

Somehow, it makes sense to me that the children would serve as a bridge to this consciousness. Could the communication within this article (like a code with an unlocking ability) act as a conduit to reconnect us to an ancient knowing lying dormant within us all? Could this ancient technology be one of love and belief?

The message continued to flow as we arrived home from *Earthdance*. I found myself running into the house to get pen and paper. I breathed calmly and deeply, allowing the communication to continue to flow. Scraps of paper were all around our living room and kitchen as I wrote and wrote. It felt like a mystery ... like trying to find a hidden treasure by putting the clues together. I scribbled geometric shapes, intriguing images, numbers, and phrases. Then, I heard a voice urging me to tune into the television. We hardly ever have the TV on, but Brian had just flipped it on to catch the late night news as we walked into the house.

Instantly, a commercial came on with the slogan: "See the World in a Whole New Way." As our daughter slept, I copied that phrase into my journal then continued to write, while lying in front of the TV. My hand became quite relaxed even though I was writing very quickly. For some reason—as though I were being guided—I drew a tail (like on the letter "y") on the bottom of the "w" in the word "way." I felt, or somehow I knew, that there was a message in this. I read the phrase again and again; I just couldn't figure out the "w." Then, like a ton of bricks, it hit. I got it. My body trembled as I said under my breath, "See the World in a Whole New Yahweh." Ah, blessed suspension, indeed.

A mystery—was it a mystery? Yes ... instantly I heard, or got, or ... something, *"We need to treat every child as though he is holy—a golden child; as if he is the baby Jesus, Yahweh! In fact, we are all Holy Children. We must only remember and believe (be-love) that this is so. From this place, the whole world will be healed. It must begin, now!"* I felt as though this was the common thread that would be present throughout the communication I was receiving.

I jumped to my feet, closed my eyes, and immediately felt the impulse to pray and reconnect with the grid of love and peace we had just sent around the world as participants of *Earthdance.* As a couple, Brian and I have hosted prayer circles in the past, and truly believe in the power of prayer ... but, in that instant, I felt the reality of divine intervention on a much deeper level.

After a few brief moments, I opened my eyes and found myself staring out our patio door. Tears poured down my cheeks as I rubbed my eyes over and over. Right there, in front of me, through many layers (smudges from Shanti's little hands on the glass door, the glare in the glass itself, branches from a tree, and a light in the distance which appeared to be coming from deep within the mountains less than two miles away) was an image of Jesus—Yahweh! It looked strikingly similar to the Shroud of Turin!

My mind was racing as it took me halfway around the globe to Baghdad where, twelve hours earlier, Jimmy had led the prayer vigil that coincided with *Earthdance.* I sent him love and mentally surrounded him with angels as he was preparing for his flight back to the states. I questioned, once again: I wonder what other work we will be doing with Jimmy?

I checked on our daughter who was still sleeping soundly. It was unusual for her to take such a long nap. I started to really believe that maybe she was working with us somehow. Perhaps she was sending the ideas, or providing the necessary space to allow all of this to come in and be processed. Suddenly, I got a flash of various dreams and coincidences Brian and I have had that included Jimmy—many of which happened before we met. I felt as if I were seeing a big picture of the situation from above. The only problem was that it felt like there was so much space between the pieces of the puzzle that was keeping me from putting it all together. I offered up to the universe that if we were supposed to do some sort of work together to assist the children, to please let it come and I would do my best to listen. I continued to journal small downloads as they came, unaware that an answer would be manifesting so quickly.

Weeks later, we were having dinner with Jimmy and another dear friend, Mishi. The conversation turned to Mishi and her relationship with our daughter, Shanti. "Aunt Mishi" had gotten to know her quite well, as she stayed with our family for a couple weeks while transitioning between habitudes. During her stay with us, Mishi gave Shanti an interesting nickname: "Little Wizard" (shortly after watching the Harry Potter movie). The moniker seemed very appropriate for such an inquisitive little being with wise old eyes, eyes that Aunt Mishi called planet eyes. Mishi would often hand her a magic marker and say, "Okay, wave your wand as you look at me through those big blue orbs, Little Wizzzzard!" Even Grandpa Bob thought the name fit! It seemed to match her personality to a "t."

During dinner, our conversation continued to dance around the topic of amazing children, as Shanti waved excitedly to a friend that the three of us did not see. It was at that time that Jimmy mentioned a new book that he was working on. It was a book about raising psychic children. We talked about kids doing things with their minds, like bending spoons and moving small objects, sending messages with their minds, and the like. This was an interesting topic to us, as we had been wondering about some of the communication our own Little Wizard seemed to be giving us. Then, Jimmy threw out the idea of us writing an article for the book. Immediately, we felt in our hearts that the shoe fit, as if it were meant to be. We were not experiencing the bending of utensils by our infant, but we were experiencing the expansion of our minds that she seemed to be part of.

On the ride home after dinner, I couldn't help but wonder: Is this all coincidence, or is it really divine guidance from the children? I asked Brian if he thought these children were communicating in some way with one another, and then sending messages out to the world around them. "It's all pretty trippy, but I'm open to the possibilities. Fasten your seat belt, sweetie!" my husband blurted from the front seat.

The more we thought about the idea of openly sharing our experiences, the more the mind chatter came in: fear, doubt, and even skepticism. "Can you imagine what my friends and family in Richfield (the town where Brian was raised) would think about me referring to my daughter, or even myself, as psychic?" Brian chuckled as we bounced up the stairs leading to our front door. He put the sleeping Little Wizard in her crib and zipped up her purple jammies. He continued to laugh out loud as he grabbed the dictionary—it's never far away, as we often research words that appear to have a different meaning depending on the person who is using them!

Webster's Seventh New Collegiate Dictionary gives the following meaning for the word "psychic": *from Greek psychikos meaning 'of the soul'; 1: of or relating to the psyche; 2: lying outside the sphere of physical science or knowledge: immaterial, moral, or spiritual in origin or force; 3: sensitive to nonphysical or supernatural forces or influences.*

Ah, yes ... the shoe did indeed fit!

Days later, while I played with Shanti before her afternoon nap, I tossed around some ideas for the article Jimmy asked us to write. We danced together while we listened to some music tapes that Grandma Pat had given her. The song, "I'm a Little Tea Pot," came on. I wondered about the intent or the meaning behind the song. I had heard it dozens of times before, yet now I was wondering: Is there a message or is it just a silly song? I looked forward to the day our daughter could talk, in order to hear her words of wisdom about questions such as this. Our little girl soon grew tired from all the singing and dancing. She crawled up in my lap to nurse, as she often does before taking a nap. I closed my eyes and the song immediately began playing over and over in my head:

"I'm a little teapot; yes, it's true
Here's an example of what I can do
I can turn my handle into a spout
Tip me over and pour me out."

Just as quickly as it began, the song stopped. Then, in my head, I heard: *This song is about being a vessel. In a sense, we are all really just jars of clay, molded into something special by our maker. When we allow ourselves to be opened, then filled, and even emptied from time to time, we are more available for Service.*

It was as if the most innocent, most graceful voice was speaking to me. Just then, I realized that I might actually be seeing the song through the eyes of a child. Perhaps the children were making this possible! At that very moment, our little one stretched her body out wide, gave me a smile, and went back to her snack. Just another quirky coincidence?

I felt expanded in the space that I knew to be my mind, yet I was fully connected with my heart. It was as if my mind was stretching in order to allow a bigger picture to reveal itself ... a picture that felt like love. I felt as though someone was calling me to *be* a vessel—to help get a message delivered. I reached a point where it seemed like I was sharing that space with another. I shook my head and, upon looking down, I noticed that our daughter had fallen asleep in my lap.

Could she really be sending some of these thoughts I wondered to myself? I realized that I often seem to get these profound ideas when she is sleeping or in deep playtime, not directly interacting with me on the physical level. It seemed very similar to experiences I encountered when she was in the womb.

This made me think about the vessel I had been during pregnancy. As Shanti slept, I noticed her journal propped up on a shelf next to me. It's filled with stories and reflections from before and after birth that would hopefully someday give her insight into her early stages of life. This gave me an idea! I surmised that maybe we could entertain the idea of pre-birth and early infant communication in the article Jimmy had asked us to write!

Coincidentally—or not—Jimmy phoned later that very day and I immediately told him that some things had been coming for the article, and that we felt very drawn to the project. He said that he felt similarly, and wanted to share an idea that had come to him. "What do you think about addressing the possibility of communication between us as adults and the essence or soul of the incoming child before birth, or even before conception?" he questioned. He had literally taken the words right out of my mouth! It was as if he had been granted access to my mind!

∞∞∞

Life with our Little Wizard has fostered in us a mindfulness of interacting with her whole being, her total self—even that part of her that is beyond the physical. We share the following journal entries—which are true accounts—in order to paint a picture of possibilities that we believe exist for communing with your child on a soul level ... not only as an infant, but before birth, and even prior to conception. Whether our daughter was and/or is helping in spirit by amplifying our own intuition, or directly intervening as an angel of sorts, we truly don't need to know. We simply need to be love, to believe.

Part of the beauty that exists in the experience of life is not knowing, and also being okay with that. However, we can't help but think there *has* to be something to all of this. Our intent in sharing our personal experiences is to open your mind and heart to the possibilities of the miracles that the kids seem to be bringing to our world. Brian likes to remind people that it's okay if they don't completely resonate with ideas like this; he says that all that is required of us at this point is that we stay open to the possibilities, for it is in this very openness that we can be most profoundly affected.

∞∞∞

I often use angel cards as a source of personal inspiration during prayer and meditation. I also use them when I am preparing to journal my thoughts for personal reflection. In my current practice as an Intuitive, I often use angel cards when doing angel readings for clients. Though it appears that the universal law of like attracts like most often prevails when pulling cards for others, I find that it is common to doubt the messages when I pull cards for myself. In a journal entry about ten months prior to the birth of our child (with no conscious idea that a pregnancy was coming), I wrote the following entry in my journal:

March 22, 2001 journal entry

Dear God and the Angels,

What should I know now that my latest creative project has been completed?

The cards I pulled were: **miracles**, **children** and **intention**. What I heard was: *The miracles are already here! You just can't see the big picture yet. Just listen and you will know. This is a time for nurturing. Focus on co-creating. Is this a time for working on artistic endeavors, or does this speak to a desire for having children?*

I didn't take the message too seriously. Perhaps the **children** card means I should focus on my inner child, I thought. I decided to release the idea to God and the universe. If it were meant to be a message for me, it would come back.

∞∞∞

One morning, a week later, I repeatedly saw myself working at an outside table, under a huge shade tree at a Starbucks down the street from our home. I couldn't get that vision out of my head, so I decided to follow intuition. I packed my things and was ready to head out to the door when a client called. Suzanne wanted to meet right away and suggested Starbucks ... *that* Starbucks! What a strange synchronicity, I thought to myself. Before leaving the house, I felt compelled to see if the angels had an additional message for me.

March 29, 2001 journal entry
(still prior to conception)

Dear Guardian Angel,

What should I know as I open to intuition this day?

I pulled the **nature**, **answered prayer** and **new love** cards. The message came through loud and clear: *Get outside today. The fresh air of nature and a change of environment will help you to breathe in new ideas. Your prayers are answered. Just be. A feeling of a new chapter or new project is in the air. Be aware of what the universe is placing before you.*

With that, I offered the following prayer:

> Dear God,
>
> Thank you for the opportunity to help Suzanne. I know that it is in giving that we truly receive. I will be open to the wisdom you may be sending through my experience with her. I also ask for guidance dealing with the abdominal cramps I've felt over the last few months. Louise Hay's book, Heal Your Body, relates this with fear and stopping the process of life. I affirm that I trust the process of life. I know that I am safe in your hands.
>
> Amen.

When I arrived at the coffee shop, I felt the impulse to pull additional cards for myself in order to continue the flow of information through journaling.

> Is there anything else I should keep in mind?

I pulled the **creativity** card.

Keep the focus of abundant energy flowing through your being, I sensed. I wanted a more specific message, so I kept on.

> Is there more that I should know about Answered Prayer?

Shuffling the cards over and over again, I pulled the **chil-**

dren, **intentions** and **new beginnings** cards. I immediately felt what some call a block. My body and mind became rigid as my soul spoke a truth. "No," I said under my breath. "Really? Kids? Now?"

If I were doing a reading for a client, my intuition would tell me that on some level, the person desired to have a child. I wondered if this was my imagination. I heard a voice inside my head: *Are you running away from something? Nurture! Explore patterns you may have in this area.*

I found myself staring off into space. I brought my gaze into focus and saw several children playing in the coffee shop, which was unusual for this particular time of day, as it was right in the middle of a school day. Hmmm ... another sign sent to provide comfort? I smiled. Then, I overhead a woman a few tables away say to friend, "Did your sister have her baby yet?"

I believe that overhearing someone saying something that sounds like it could be a coincidental clue to you is one form of clairaudience, or clear hearing. Could it be that the universe just spoke through someone else for me to hear? I wondered. I decided to continue, as the synchronicities were piling up.

What else should I know?

Intentions, **body care**, **spiritual growth**, and **divine timing** came next. In my heart, I instantly knew what this meant, but could hardly believe the words were coming so clearly. *You have fears to face dealing with having children and your own inner child. Do not run away from the fear. You need to deal with this for your own health and well-being. This is all a part of your growth on your path. Trust. Let go and let God. This is all Divine Timing.*

While processing this information, I felt the irresistible urge to have a child. When I saw the **divine timing** card, I felt a strong sensation, similar to the feeling that you get when you reconnect with someone whom you have not seen in a long time. With my logical mind protesting, I thought: Could it be that one of the angels talking to me was in actuality a soul that was ready to come in though us? Or, was my mind playing tricks on me?

I decided I had had enough offbeat messages for one day,

so while I waited for Suzanne, I started reading a book I brought along. I only had time to read a few pages, but they were very telling. The primary focus dealt with the idea of people showing up in your life as mirrors to the self. It also suggested that whenever you help someone or give council on a particular situation, what you share relates in some way to what you are going through yourself.

I wondered what questions Suzanne would have for her reading. I looked up and heard Suzanne say, "Oh, I'm so glad you could meet with me at the last minute. I have something on my mind that I can't seem to shake. I was told that I can't have children, but I really want them. I was hoping that you could give me your intuitive read on the situation." I took a deep breath, hugged her, and smiled.

The process of the universe (or our incoming child) sending me clues continued the following week while we were visiting our dear friends, Alex and Simone. "Oh, Thereeza," chirped Simone in her native South African tongue, "I have something for you." We laid down our kitchen towels as she handed me a small envelope. "It spoke to me when I was in the checkout line at the grocery store, and I just knew you were to have it. I don't know why!" she added after a brief pause.

I handed the envelope to Brian, begging him to open it. I was definitely feeding off of Simone's giddiness, even though I still had no clue what was unfolding before us. Inside the envelope was a small greeting card. The card, by Anne Geddes, was blank on the inside ... the message for us was the image on the front cover. Grinning at us was a picture of a naked baby girl, lying amongst dozens of beautiful pink roses. Her smile was so cheeky that she could barely open her eyes.

∞∞∞

Like layers of an onion, I spent the next couple weeks going deeper and deeper within myself. I peeled and peeled, and I was finally faced with the realization that there were issues hiding at my core that had a stronger hold on me than I was aware of. I was allowing fear to overpower me, just like the pungent, yet slightly sweet aroma of an onion is apt to do. The idea of a certain incoming soul interacting with me still glimmered—a companion, dancing with me through the process.

Knowing that facing fears is such a profound conduit for growth, I decided to face mine, head on. Once again, I had no idea the ride I was in for!

I decided to have a full moon ceremony to release the fears that kept creeping into my mind. I wrote the following message on a piece of paper that I would later burn:

> *I release any fears dealing with my birth mother search, having my own children, the fear of dying giving birth, fear of motherhood, etc.*
> *I invite the guidance and comfort of God, the angels, (and a certain potential soul if you are out there).*

I burned my prayer paper in our backyard fireplace while in the company of a small group of friends. I focused my mind on women giving birth at that time all over the planet; my own parents; my birthparents; those finding challenges conceiving; and the list went on. In the middle of the night, hours after our full moon ceremony, I was awakened from a deep sleep. I felt a presence that seemed to be hovering over our bed. I did not see her face outside of my mind's eye, but I believed her to be the Blessed Mother Mary. She said nothing, but I felt an embrace as she gave me some kind of message. Then she turned as if she was welcoming another presence. As I type this, I remember it like it was just yesterday. I felt a sense of child-like faith and love emanating from this energy.

Was this energy some kind of guardian angel? Was it the energy of our future child? I felt that they were somehow giving me what I needed, energetically, in order to release my fears as I felt an invisible bubble coming from them and surrounding me. The bubble remained from that moment on, weaving itself in and out of my consciousness.

On Easter morning, one week after my full moon prayer, Brian and I traveled to Sedona, Arizona for an Easter meal with friends. Our celebration included a healing time for each one of us. A friend guided us through meditation as we each took turns focusing intentions on one another.

When it was my turn, I offered a message to any potential incoming souls, expressing the question of my readiness (while Brian shared the focus in his own mind). Instantly, I got a vision of a single dolphin in my mind, jumping out of the water again and again. During Brian's meditation, he saw a bookcase containing a book with a blank cover. He held the book to his chest to discern the title of the book. He said aloud, "Christo." After the meditation, Brian told me that he felt as if we would have a child some day and something about the child would deal with Christo. Crazy as it sounds, a dear friend then shared that whenever we got around to having a child, we might want to be mindful in approaching the experience as if we were Mary and Joseph bringing in this child.

It is only now, in writing this, that I understand the message more clearly. It is the same message that came the night of *Earthdance*. It is a message to all parents and caregivers. We are to minister to the children as if they are divine; and in this, they shall minister to us the same.

Before we left the Easter gathering, we sat in a circle chanting, "Shanti, Shanti, Shanti Om," which is a phrase that invokes the creation of inner peace in the Sanskrit language. With Brian sitting directly behind me, our bodies touching, holding hands, I felt the vibration of the sound resonate in my tummy as we chanted in unison. I imagined singing and chanting these very words during childbirth someday.

Days later, I realized that I was a couple days late getting my period this time around. I wondered if my body was playing tricks on me, so I decided to pray in order to get a read on the situation. Feeling in tune with Mother Nature, I grabbed my deck of Animal Medicine cards along with my journal.

April 16, 2001 journal entry

"What should I know about being late with my cycle?"

I pulled the **dolphin** card. (Remember, this is a true story!) I gasped as I remembered the vision I had of a jumping dolphin on Easter. *Listen to your body rhythms and the creation within you,* I heard. *A new phase in your life is emerging. Something dealing with the earth's children is ahead. In addition to children, this relates to your life path more than you know at this time.* Then I pulled the ***snake*** card. *It is a time for pro-creation and transformation. This is much bigger than you can imagine.*

∞∞∞

We had been pondering the idea of selling our house, along with most of our bulky possessions, and planned to travel abroad for several months to just "be" and reflect. One thing we were to reflect on while away would be having a child. After pulling the **dolphin** card, I decided to get the "For Sale by Owner" sign the next day. I went to the store and spent quite a bit of time trying to find the sign I had in mind. Funny, they didn't seem to have what I was envisioning. I hastily grabbed one anyhow, and walked toward the cashier. About half way to the checkout, I was stopped in my tracks. An image flashed in my head. I saw myself at the checkout counter with a pregnancy test in hand. To my surprise, I grabbed a test kit (the kind that had two tests for security!) and headed for the check out.

While driving home, I still sensed the bubble around me; the one that came in the middle of the night on Easter. It felt as strong as ever. I began having a conversation with it in my mind. "Okay. I got a test. Is that what you wanted me to do?" Just saying that gave me a secret sense of joy. We wanted to be conscious parents, and were waiting until the right time; we were waiting to be guided. But, I didn't imagine that time being so soon.

I got home and found myself slowly reading the box. I remembered back to the wonderful evening a few weeks prior when we spent the night under jasmine and honeysuckle blossoms from our garden that I wove into the canopy of our bed. I felt that conception, when we were truly ready, would be a moment of that kind of mindfulness. Finally taking my blinders off, I thought:

Could we have conceived *that* night? I was only a couple of days late, which was not really all that uncommon. With a child-like grin, I ripped open the kit and ran to the bathroom. Suddenly, what I was fearful of gave me a sense of great joy.

Waiting for the required ten minutes seemed like an eternity. Images of the last few weeks' episodes were flashing in my head: the full moon ceremony ... the Easter meditations ... the card readings ... the bubble. The reality of it all was mind-boggling. One thing that I did know as I stood there waiting for the results was that I wanted to be pregnant. In a weird way, I felt like the bubble I was feeling was the soul of our future child. It felt like a movie, but it felt so real. I bent down to peak at the tester's result window. I closed my eyes and smiled. Wow. This could be a book, I thought. I called Brian at work and told him to come home for lunch. The rest of the day is a blessed blur.

April 18, 2001 journal entry

I am immediately pulling cards after getting consecutive "positive" results on BOTH my home pregnancy tests!

Snake (again): A time of pro-creation, transformation. **Dolphin** (again!) reminding me: Listen to the rhythms of creation within you. Last, while asking for additional guidance, I got **courage**: Think, say, and do what you believe.

That night, after learning that we were pregnant, Brian was reading a book before bed. It just so happened that the section he was reading was about dolphins actually assisting in the human birthing process! It was an idea that was new to us, hard to believe. The idea of dolphins as midwives awakened us to find out what it was that we did believe, so we could think, say, and do it!

∞∞∞

The next few months we found ourselves learning everything we could take in about the experience of birth. We felt that newborn babies were fully sentient beings, aware of everything going on around them during the birthing process. We wondered if practices such as ultrasound, anesthetics, and bright lighting had an effect on the spiritual DNA of a newly developing human being. Did it matter if the umbilical cord was cut before it stopped pulsating? What about being greeted in this new world by beings wearing masks and then being separated from the one whom we were in such close union with for nine months? What was this gentle, natural birth we were hearing of? We decided to let our hearts lead our discernment.

"Wow. There is an actual doctor in Russia who has done over 20,000 water births, honey!" my husband shouted from the den.

"Were they all with dolphins?" I queried from the kitchen. Intrigued, I decided to join him. I walked into the office and found printed sheets of paper all over the room.

"No, not all of them, but get this!" Brian said excitedly. "This website says that a woman was giving birth in the Black Sea and a small group of dolphins came up to her. They pushed the doctor and bystanders away, and apparently did something with their sonar up and down her body. The mother had no pain during the birth. The child was found later to have an unusually high IQ."

I organized our research into a binder, as we were seriously interested in the idea of a waterbirth. When we went to bed that evening, I put my hand on my tummy, and sent a mental thought to the little one growing inside. "If you would like to come into this world in the water, please let us know. We are listening."

A couple weeks later, our friends, Kay and Tom surprised us with a phone call from the airport. Due to a flight change, they would have a layover in our city. They wanted to visit and drop off a gift that they picked up while recently in Hawaii. Sitting on our loveseat, we opened the small package. Kay and Tom looked on, waiting for our response. After unwrapping the last piece of tissue paper, Brian held up a beautiful, crystal figurine of a dolphin mother and her baby. "We swam with the dolphins on our trip. For some reason, we kept thinking of you when we were with them!" Kay explained. "We were in a gift shop after spending the morning with the dolphins, and this piece just called to us. You are supposed to have it!" We took this as confirmation that our baby would be born in the water. Our friends were not surprised to hear that we were just reading about dolphins as midwives, communing with human mothers and their babies. Kay snickered, jabbing her elbow into Tom, and said, "Guess those dolphins knew exactly what they were doing when they prompted us to bring that little trinket for these two!"

∞∞∞

The idea of communing with our unborn child in an energetic manner was introduced to us during our first trimester of pregnancy. We had also read that the soul actually merges with the physical body at some time during the pregnancy. As a way of welcoming the soul's merge, we had a ceremony when we were three months along. We envisioned white light surrounding both of our hearts. Then we sent this light to the womb. From the womb, we sent white light out into the universe to the incoming soul, inviting it into our family, and also welcoming further communication.

Two weeks later, we settled in at our kitchen table for a little a date with a deck of cards. It had been a long day full of baby errands and work in the nursery. We finally sat down at around 9 p.m. to play a card game. In the middle of our first hand, I felt an extremely powerful presence. I wondered if it could be the baby's soul. Brian immediately felt the presence, too. It was so strong that he got goose bumps over his whole body. It was the first time I saw him have them on his face. It was such a profound new feeling that I automatically resorted to fear and grabbed my rosary. It was a very special rosary given to Shanti, in utero, from Tracie, one of her godmothers. Remembering it was from Medjugorje, I called to the Blessed Mother for protection. (I laugh as I look back upon this now.) Then our dog, started barking and running around in circles the way he does when someone comes in that he has a special connection with; he was obviously excited, but not at all scared. Brian noted the way the dog was behaving and told me that there was nothing to be afraid of.

I told Brian that I felt at least two different energies. I wondered if one could be the incoming soul, and the other my birth great-grandmother (I was once told by an Intuitive that my great grandmother, from birth, was one of my guardian angels. She supposedly had dark hair and wore it up in a bun.). Before going to bed, I prayed and said that I was open to any work that we were to do together if it was for the good of all.

I woke the next morning feeling very strange. I had vivid dreams that were still calling to me. I remembered that during my dream, I had vivid communication with Doreen Virtue (a person who taught me to talk with the angels), James Twyman (whom we didn't know personally at the time), and my mother and father. It was like we were working on some kind of project together that dealt with children (this was before Jimmy's published work with the psychic children.) Though it didn't make much sense, it felt like some kind of completion had occurred that I was not able to explain. I felt good. Confused, but good.

Later that morning, as Brian was putting finishing touches on his paint job in the baby's room, the phone rang. A woman on the line wasted no words explaining that she was a volunteer for a national reunion agency. She had just spoken to my mother, as I had her listed as a contact person on a website dedicated to reunions." I immediately knew what was happening. I cried out loud, "Oh, my God!" Tears of gratitude rolled down my face. The woman shared that my mom was the most understanding and loving adoptive parent she had ever spoken to during a pre-reunion call.

I said, "Yes. My Mom *is* an angel. My mother told me that she believed in her heart that a reunion would take place before our baby was born so that the circle would be complete—like the child would be helping to orchestrate it all, behind the scenes." Having had the opportunity to experience the feeling of what it was like not to be able to have biological children of her own, I knew the healing would be for all of us, if a reunion came to pass before the birth.

The woman on the other line said, "It's wonderful that you call your Mom an angel. Can I ask you a question? Do you really believe in angels?"

I laughed as I cried and said, "I sure do."

"It's so good to hear you say that!" she said. " I do, too!"

I heard my birthmother Carol's voice for the first time on the phone about an hour later. She said that she had gotten the idea the night before (can you guess the approximate time?) of entering her own name into a specific search engine on the Internet, as she felt the presence of her deceased grandmother guiding her. I asked her if the grandmother she was referring to happened to have dark hair that she wore in a bun. Carol exclaimed, "Yes! How did you know that?"

I was wondering if that little soul of ours could be helping to orchestrate this while still in spirit, as I heard Carol say, "Have you recently had a child or are you currently with child? I had a feeling one of these had to be true, because I feel a child-like energy around you, even though we haven't yet met."

I was already in a state of shock when Carol continued by saying, "Theresa, I hope you don't think I'm crazy, but there's a weird question I've been waiting to ask you." Without pausing she asked, "Are you psychic? I mean, do you communicate with angels or do things with your mind, or anything? It probably sounds really weird, but I've been called psychic before, and I was wondering if you were aware of having a similar gift, too?" I raised my eyebrows in amazement.

After this initial phone call, Brian and I hugged as we plopped down on the couch. We shared our bewilderment at the chain of events that seemed to be unfolding. In the wonder of it all, we couldn't help but feel the involvement of a special little angel whose room we had just finished decorating as a symbol of welcoming.

∞∞∞

December hit, and our child's birth was only a few weeks away! I decided to grab a blanket and take a nap on the floor of her bedroom to further connect with her energy. When I woke, I felt very drawn to watch *A Christmas Box,* a video that came to us years ago as a special gift from my parents. The intensity of this gift was taken to a new level as we watched it this night. There is a special part in the storyline where one of the characters realizes the very first gift of Christmas. The character explains, "...for God so loved the world that he gave His only Son." As he explained this, two things happened. The first was that Brian noticed the time on the clock. The numbers on the clock were the very same numbers that make up the month and day in our anniversary date. When we see this number, we take it as a sign that we are being blessed with a synchronicity that deals with our purpose together. The second thing that happened was that I could feel the baby dancing inside me as if it were happy or excited!

"I wonder if, somehow, our work together may have something to do with the gift of a child," Brian said.

I answered him, "And isn't it just too weird that all of these messages are coming as we are awaiting the birth of our own child?"

"Do you think we'll be helping children ... or maybe families who are expecting children?" I noticed the tape counter on the VCR. It read 411 — another sign! As people sometimes use the code number 411 to speak of someone's location, we take this number to be communication that we are to be involved in a center or 'place' to do work involving children.

∞∞∞

Our daughter was born during the week of Christmas in a free-standing birth center. Our midwife, Lylaine, was completely open to the new children coming in at this time. Most of the labor occurred in the familiarity of our home. When the actual birth was close at hand, I phoned Lylaine to see if she thought it was time to go to the center. She firmly, but lovingly explained, "You will need to go within. Use your intuition to really connect with the baby. The baby will tell you when it is time." Soon after, the energy that I called the bubble grew in intensity, and I knew it was time.

We got to the birth center in perfect time to slip into the water and assist our daughter in her birth. Our little dolphin was birthed with candlelight and a recording of dolphin sounds as we chanted Shanti, Shanti, Shanti Om. The three of us were at home, tucked into our own bed, four hours later.

It was customary for a nurse to do a home visit within 24 hours of the birth. One of the nurses called to explain that the birth center was overloaded by an abundance of babies wanting to come in during the holy season. She was having a hard time getting to all of her home visits, and was wondering how we were doing. The nurse shared that she heard about our pregnancy and birth experience, and figured we were doing fine since it seemed that we knew how to communicate with our new family member. We explained that it was really our daughter doing the great job during her transition. We were just doing our best to listen.

We continued to foster a gentle transition to life outside the womb. Soft sound effects played throughout our dimly lit house: recordings of ocean waves, dolphin sounds, soft native flute, and the human heartbeat. We gave our daughter gentle massage and reiki and maintained skin-to-skin contact between mom, dad, and baby on a regular basis. We held the intention of connecting to her beyond her physical body, seeing her as bigger than she appeared, and letting her know this.

We gave our daughter her first real bath during her second week of life, when my parents were in town to visit. It was so special to me that they not only bought her baby bathtub, but that they were present to witness the event. As we drew the bath water, Brian had an idea: Why don't we baptize her during her first bath? He lit a large bundle of sweet sage and allowed the smoke to gently dance as it cleansed the room. We filled her tub with warm water and placed it on our bed. We lit candles and each took a turn sharing a special message.

Grandpa Bob, a deacon in the Catholic faith community, spoke of the child coming into the world being filled with light, "May you continue to hold Christ's light in your heart." Grandma Pat offered, "You will be my teacher." She continued by sharing, "the child will lead us," as she guided Brian to place anointing oils over our daughter's heart. As our ceremony was drawing to a close, the birth center called. The midwife on the line said, "We've all been hearing about you down at the birth center and the way you communicate with your daughter. We were wondering if you'd be interested in teaching a class to expectant parents." We chuckled and said, "Sure, but our daughter will probably be the one teaching the class."

∞∞∞

I took some time off from working with clients to really be present for our little one. When our daughter was a few months old, a woman came to me seeking guidance. I felt that the time might be right to work with clients again, and I decided to let this reading serve as an indicator. The young woman told me that she wanted to know if she would find her soulmate. I instantly received an impression, though it had nothing to do with a soulmate. I asked the woman, "Does the name Isaiah mean anything to you?"

Tears welled up in her eyes, and she looked as though a heavy weight had been taken off her shoulders. She explained that she had lost a baby before birth, and that she had named the baby to help her with the grieving process. The name she chose was Isaiah. No one knew about the name, and she took this as a sign that there really was a form of existence before birth. She shared that this gave her much comfort and renewed faith. The woman asked me to continue with her reading as she still wanted guidance regarding her soulmate. I glanced down at my daughter who was playing with a velvet bag that contained angel cards that I hadn't used in some time. I took this as communication from her that the time might be right to begin using them again. I shuffled this deck of cards and through teary eyes pulled, **child**, **guardian angel**, and **soulmate**. We both felt that she had a special little child, an angel if you will, illuminating her path.

Since the conception of our daughter, we have had so many profound experiences like this one that seem to involve the children. They have become an integral component in our lives. As a result, we are approaching everyday life in a way that can best be described as "beyond the physical." We believe that support, connection, and communication exist in ways that we are only beginning to comprehend. And we feel love at the base of it all.

This reminds me of something my brother, Mark, once told me. Though in his early thirties at the time, he explained quite passionately that he felt as though he were really still a child at heart, almost as if he were a child stuck in an adult body, complete with manufactured responsibilities. He said, "When we were kids, we were *real*." It makes me wonder what our world would be like if we were all as in tune with our inner child as my brother Mark; always honoring the imagination and limitless belief of our child self.

I can't help but feel that the real message from the children is that each and every day can be *real*. Every day can be filled with love, joy, and peace ... but only if we choose this collectively. As I type, I can hear a verse from a song playing in my mind, *Blessed be the peacemakers, for they shall be called the children of God...* Is it possible that the kids are showing us how to create a shift right now? Are they showing us how to truly see, hear, feel, and know what is real?

I believe that deep within each one of us lies a universal truth: We all exist beyond our physical bodies. We are all psychic children. We can all communicate in a way that is real by using our hearts to transcend our often-limiting minds. The heart is the most accurate channel for all of the senses!

As I search for a conclusion to this article, our daughter is climbing up into my lap. She is grabbing at a stone on my necklace and reminding me of an incident that happened just last week. We were attending a going away party for some friends. While at the party, our daughter sat mesmerized by an amethyst crystal pendant that one of the women wore around her neck. The woman took off the amethyst nugget and dangled it in front of our daughter, who put her hand out and delicately pinched the air in several places, within about two inches of the gemstone. I was confused by her actions as I had witnessed her manipulate very small objects with precision over the past several months.

Another partygoer said, "Oh, look ... she sees the energy around the crystal and is confused because her fingers are going right through it." This possibility had not even occurred to me.

I quickly followed our daughter's lead, and communicated to her that I understood by putting my fingers near the piece of amethyst. I stopped in the area that she stopped, and made eye contact with her while keeping my fingers in place. Then, I slowly extended my fingers further as I gently grabbed the gemstone. She looked at me curiously, and then did the same thing with her own fingers. Upon touching the amethyst, she crawled into my lap, gave me solid, knowing eye contact, followed by a gentle kiss of affirmation. She smiled *big*, and let out her signature laugh (we actually call it a clicking) that sounds very much like a dolphin's sound. It was as if she had seen something for the first time, then suddenly remembered it was not new at all.

With that, the Little Wizard seems to be sharing a message: Things aren't always as they seem to be ... our hearts know what is real. This is not something we need to learn; rather, something we need only to remember. Believe ... be love.

Theresa Stuesser has a B.S. in education from the University of Wisconsin–Platteville. Her graduate studies involved integrated instruction and the whole child. She served as a consultant for the Wisconsin Department of Public Instruction and was a pioneer in the charter school movement in Arizona. Theresa has 17 years of child development experience in outdoor education/camp programming, as an elementary school teacher, and as an assistant principal, specializing in curriculum. She is a certified Angel Therapy Practitioner by Dr. Doreen Virtue, and currently serves clients worldwide as an Intuitive doing personal readings. She also lectures and offers workshops on angelic communication and self-development. Theresa and her husband, Brian, co-created Angels of Ashland, which facilitates community events to foster spiritual growth and raise consciousness. Contact Info: Angels of Ashland, P.O. Box 3552, Ashland, OR 97520, USA, >www.angelsofashland.com<.

3.

We do not belong to you.
I think you already know that.
But we have come to you,
As you!
Does that make sense?
The Children would not be in this world today
If it wasn't for the work you have already done.
You have welcomed us,
And now we are here.
You have called us by the love you have shown one another.
And now you are being loved.

Don't try to understand this with your mind,
But See it with your heart.
Then you will know that it is true.
Then you will believe it.

4.

We are the reflection of your love,
Your Light,
And your Grace.
We are the perfection of your highest vision
Of who you can be,
And who you already are.
You can teach us so much by realizing this.
And we can teach you as well.
We are here to create a New World together,
A world that has always existed in the Mind of God.
But now you must allow it to exist in your mind.
Then it will be seen and experienced.
It can't happen any other way.

The children that are being born today are no different
Than any other child.
It is simply time.
Do you understand yet?

5.

Now is the time that you decided to remember who you are.
This is the moment when everything can change for you.
The children's mission is to show you what that will look like.
If you look into our eyes then you will know.
If you are willing to lay aside your fear for a moment,
And really look,
Then you will see something you have hidden from till now.
You will see yourself.
Your Self!
And we will smile at you,
For in that moment everything will make perfect sense.

We must work together for this to happen,
And that is why we are offering this book.
We want you to understand us better
So you will be able to help us fulfill our mission.

6.

Now I will define our mission for you.

We are here to show you the truth that has always been true.

You are loved by God!

That's it.

Are you willing to allow it to be that simple?

7.

And we need you as well if we are to achieve the highest
vision
We are capable of achieving.
Just remember that you are not doing this for us
As much as you're doing it for yourself.

What you give to me
Is received by thee.

This is your chance to be born again,
And to be raised in a way that will lead to your Perfect Life.
If you are willing to learn this,
And give it to the children that are around you now,
Then you will receive it yourself.
That is the gift you will give us,
And we will give it back to you.
Then you will remember.

8.

We are all Psychic Children.
Here is the first lesson I can teach you:

Don't try to define if your children are psychic or not.
Let go of those labels.
Simply know that God dwells within them perfectly,
This and every moment.
God's gifts are theirs,
And they are yours as well.
Treat them as if they possess all the power in the Universe.
They do.
Act as if they possess all the love in the Universe.
They do.
Remember that the gifts you give them
You yourself will receive.
Give them everything,
And you will have everything.

Once again,
Are you willing to allow it to be this simple?

9.

If you realize that all the advice we offer about raising
Psychic Children is really about you,
Then you learn this lesson very well.
But if you insist that your children are separate from you,
Then you will miss the real lesson.

We are going to tell you many things about what we need,
But you need these things too.
Open your mind now to include more than you believe,
And you will see that belief has no role to play here.
Love is the only lesson we will teach,
And it doesn't know anything about the differences you
see.
It sees you as God Sees You.

And that is the real goal.
You are here to do the same.

Good Advice on Raising Psychic Children

By Valerie Thea Vandermeer

Bless you for the path you have chosen. Your challenges are great and many. Your rewards will be deep. You will be misunderstood by others, yet your courage and integrity will be the greatest gifts you can give your children. For in trusting your own wisdom and walking your own truth in the world, you will be a shining model for your children to emulate.

This is the core of our work then ... to do our own spiritual homework so that our children experience us living in right relationship.

Your children were born acutely aware and extraordinarily wise. They chose you to parent them. Remember that. They chose you—and they chose well. You must now put aside all the ideas you have about being a parent and simply "be" one. Parenting, all parenting, is not about doing something, it's about being. It's a state of vibration.

Highly aware children feel vibration—the entire universe pulses and hums with aliveness and our children experience this phenomenon, each in their own way. Some see colors and auras, some can hear other's thoughts, some have healing abilities, inner vision, or prophetic abilities. Some are simply aware of their deep connection to humanity with an uncanny knack for expressing it in a way that touches people's hearts. Whatever you call it, these are utterly human attributes. Everyone has the potential to experience and express all these phenomena. But most don't. To understand our children we must recognize and accept that there is a difference between undeveloped potential and actualized abilities.

It is very popular in spiritual circles to say that these children aren't different or special—that all children are endowed with these abilities simply by virtue of their humanity. This is essentially true. But it misses a vital point. All children are born with this potential, but not all children *express* these abilities. And there are differing degrees of these abilities. Just as every child can learn to play a simple tune on the piano, very few of those children will play concertos by age five. Every child experiences intuition and moments of deep knowing, magical play friends, and seeing rainbow colors floating around people. Yet, very few of those children will articulate deeply spiritual principles by age five. Highly aware children *are* different. Acknowledge them. Honor their sacred gifts. This is our path to becoming better caretakers of earth's children.

Breathe deeply, pay attention, listen to your words, feel your body. Be in the now. You must disentangle yourself from the neurological webbing that traps us like marionettes in unconscious pattern of reactive behavior. Our children feel and sense and often act out our underlying emotional issues. They quite literally "pick up" the vibration and model it for us. For us. Watch your child's behavior and quietly ask yourself, "What part of me feels this way?" Listen deeply for the answer. We can learn who we really are by watching our children closely. We can choose who we want to become. Teach your children that it's safe to change, by changing and challenging yourself.

Remember that each day, each moment, is new and ripe with unlimited potential to grow and learn together. Be responsive to the moment. Experience the truth of your deepest being with your child. Don't listen to yesterday's echoes. Draw forth the unfolding moment with more than just your eyes and ears. Slow down. Receive it through all your senses, multi-dimensionally. You cannot live as others do. Be in *your* life with *your* child.

Our children are each unique, individual and wholly complete in their own right. In our desperation to understand, to make sense with the mind, we give them labels. We try to identify them and group them together by characteristics. Psychic, Indigo, Blue Ray ... on and on we go. Even seemingly positive or prestigious labels such as these are still limiting ideas. Our children, and all humans, are limitless beings blessed with absolute transformational potential. We forget how very powerful we are. Our children are here to remind us. They remind us that ideas are rooted in memories of the past and conjecture about the future. Our children live in the present. We must gather ourselves and meet them where they are.

We see our children's brilliance—their deep inner knowing and conviction. They are "hard-wired" for the unfolding of everyday wisdom and they just follow truth where it leads them. Mirror this. Trust your own inner whisperings and follow your heart's direction. Inside each of us is a template, a pattern of faith and power and the potential of who we are and how we will appear in the world. We *know* who we are supposed to be. It is deeply embedded in the tissues of our bodies and imprinted on our souls. Truly listen and you can hear the sounds of inner wisdom, feel its vibration. When we contradict this inner guidance it's as though we are playing two disharmonic notes on an instrument. The sound is distressing to our children. They hear this sad song everywhere around them as they move through a world filled with people who have lost connection to themselves. Let them hear your soul singing.

Let yourself fail. Do it openly with grace and self forgiveness. Summon your courage and allow your children to really see you unmasked. Parenting a highly aware child demands total integrity. There is simply no other way. They can feel when the truth is not being told and it is deeply upsetting, even debilitating to them.

What a gift you give when you acknowledge your own behaviors, name them clearly, and affirm how you plan to change. This is the way we teach our children how to grow.

Embrace your authentic self and share who you are freely. Teach your children to do the same. We must respect and nurture the highly evolved sensitivities and unique intelligences of our children. Their anomalous and idiosyncratic behaviors reflect the emergence of traits more supportive of the human species than our current culturally accepted behaviors. Humanity is changing and they are a vital part of that shift. This is what they are meant to do, their purpose, a fundamental reason for their being present on the planet—to think deeply on that which has meaning, recognize truth, and stand apart in uniqueness.

Follow your children. They will lead you to other highly aware children—and then you will see magic. In their encounters, we witness human beings in authentic relationship full of bliss and joy. Watch them play and you will see them literally embodying the greatest principles of life's truths: We are all connected, we are ultimately empowered, we have all the answers within, we are safe in our bodies, we all resonate to unconditional love and acceptance, we are all perfect just as we are. Our children blossom and breathe, open and shine, in the presence of one another. They are manifesting heaven on earth as they dance and play.

As parents, we are blessed to gather round them as their caretakers and share our amazing journeys with one another. Hold hands, share tears, feel joy. Tell our stories. We are meant to be together. When we are together, deep healing occurs. Find each other.

What can we do to parent our highly aware children? We do not need to help them uncover who they are, for they have not forgotten. We do not need to teach them metaphysical principles, for they *are* those principles made manifest. Our call then as highly aware parents is to be fully present, dynamically responsive, intuitively awakened, and wholly open to these children as our teacher/learners. Support them in the emergence into this dimension of physical form with love, consideration and attention. Provide them with tools to help them relate to this world and her people. Love them unconditionally, wholly, completely. Tell them they belong here, on this earth, at this time. And learn to trust that they are certainly leading us somewhere.

Valerie Thea Vandermeer has been an intuitive healer and gifted spiritual educator for more than fifteen years. She has developed and presents a variety of workshops on healing and the body's wisdom, shamanism, meditation, enlightened corporate leadership, and the power of nature. She recently founded EarthWalk, which provides workshops and resources to support highly aware children and their families. Valerie's empowering presence invites us to express the sacred in our every day lives and to live joyously in authentic relationship with one another. For more information contact her at >earth.walk@verizon.net< or at >www.earth-walk.net<.

10.

Are you willing to realize that your child is the Christ,
Or the Buddha,
Or the Enlightened One?

This is the most important thing we can tell you
About raising a Psychic Child.
It is also the most important thing we can tell you about life.
Look for the Enlightened One in your child's eyes.
Look for the Enlightened One everywhere.
Then you will see it within yourself,
And that is the key.
Your child is here to teach you by allowing you to give.
The more you give,
The more you will realize that you already have everything.
And when you realize that you already have everything,
Then you will be able to give your child everything he needs
To grow and realize all his gifts.

11.

If you want to raise your children to be open to their gifts,
Then you must first be open to yours.

You will hear this lesson over and over in many different
ways.
You cannot give anything to your children
That you do not realize is yours.
Once you know you have it,
Then you can give it.

They are waiting for you to realize how incredible you are.
Then they will give that gift back to you.
You will receive it in every glance,
Every word they speak,
All because you were the first to be brave.

12.

Your child chose you as her parent
Because of the gifts you are capable of offering her.

Life did not begin at birth.
Nor did your relationship with your child.
It is likely that you have been here before
And chose to return at this important time.
You have so much work to do together.
There are so many things for you to discover.
You have renewed a partnership that has always existed.
If you honor it now,
Then all the gifts of the past will return to you.

13.

You have entered into a sacred union with your child.
It was chosen for you,
And by you,
Before time began.
Please try to remember this as you set about the task
Of helping your child reawaken his gifts.

14.

You must make a choice now.
Your decision extends beyond the relationship you now
enjoy.
It is a choice you will make with the whole world.
The entire universe is involved.
That is why we are working with you so closely.
It is more important than you can imagine.
As your child grows and you see the fruit of this work,
Then you will understand.
The children have come to save the world.
This is not an exaggeration.
But they need your help now.
Choose love,
And the rest will be revealed naturally.

15.

Here is the question you must ask yourself:
What is the highest gift you would choose to offer your child?

What would you have her learn that will help her
Complete her mission on earth?
What would you offer him that would change the way he
Sees the world,
And everyone in the world?

If there were only one thing you would give them,
What would it be?

16.

Here is another question for you to ask:
What is the highest gift you would choose to receive?

17.

When you set about the business of guiding your child,
You will discover that these two questions are the same.
The sooner you realize this,
The more you will be able to help awaken your child's gifts.

You are in this together.

18.

The world needs the wisdom and gifts your child can offer,
And it needs you as well.
Think of it like this:
You are having a dream and it's time to wake up.
It's time for you to be about the business
Of creating a joyous life.
When you open your eyes and look next to you
You'll see your child looking into your eyes.
You were dreaming together.
When you wake up,
She wakes up.

Now it's time to get to work.

The Following article is excerpted from The Care and Feeding of Indigo Children *by Doreen Virtue, Ph.D. (Hay House), 2001, reprinted by permission.*

NATURAL ALTERNATIVES TO RITALIN

by Doreen Virtue

It's estimated that over six million American children now take psychotropic medication for ADHD, depression, and other psychological maladies. One in every thirty-six Australian boys, in New South Wales, Australia, takes Ritalin. Ritalin is the most widely prescribed medication for children. Other commonly prescribed drugs include Dexedrine, Cylert, Tofranil, Norpamin, Prozac, and Paxil.

When an Indigo Child is labeled with having Attention Deficit Disorder (ADD) or Attention Deficit with Hyperactivity Disorder (ADHD), their inner feeling of being "different" is validated. But instead of feeling happy that they are different because of their spiritual Life's Purpose and spiritual gifts, the Indigo Child feels ashamed about their differentness.

Being put on medication is a two-fold dilemma for the Indigo Child. On the one hand, it offers them the opportunity to finally "fit in" with other kids and to please their parents and teachers. It may even give them a "high" that helps them escape the pain of feeling different, or feeling empty inside if they aren't working on their Purpose. But the price is high: their spiritual gifts will be bound in a chemical straightjacket.

An Indigo Child who takes Ritalin or other psychotropic

drugs soon loses touch with their intuition, psychic abilities, and their warrior personality. These children were sent to earth with these three spiritual gifts for the express purpose of cleaning up our planet, environmentally and socially. When we turn Indigo Children into apathetic conformists, through prescription drugs, they forget their Life's Purpose. This leads to one more generation that lets the government and the environment become sicker and more polluted.

Yes, Ritalin does work in harnessing a wild child's behavior temporarily. But, the child must then stay on the drugs for their effects to last. There are many other solutions to the temporary behavioral problems of children who are labeled ADD or ADHD. These solutions are natural, and most of them are free of charge or low charge. They will help your child to sleep, concentrate, and get along with others, better. And most importantly, these natural methods will enhance instead of hinder, your Indigo Child's Purpose and spiritual gifts.

In this article, I'll give you some basic, easy-to-do, practical solutions. I know that if I gave you a laundry list of "do this, that, this, and that" suggestions, you'd become overwhelmed. After all, studies show that ADD and ADHD run in families. Children who are ADD- or ADHD-labeled are likely to have parents whom exhibit ADD or ADHD behaviors, such as disorganization, hyperactivity, or impulsivity.

What this means to us, in reality, is that most Indigo Children are being raised by Lightworkers. Indigos and Lightworkers share some of the same characteristics of being "ungrounded" and "disorganized" on this dense earthly plane. So, it's easy for the Lightworker parents to become overwhelmed by complicated suggestions about naturally healing ADHD or ADD behavior.

If That Wasn't Bad Enough . . .

Not only do they lose sight of their spiritual gifts and Purposes, but also Indigo Children who use prescription medication have a high likelihood of using illegal drugs. Perhaps it is because those who have anxiety or depression are seeking relief. Or, perhaps it's because we are teaching our children to, "Just say 'yes' to drugs" when we send them to the school nurse's office for their daily Ritalin dosage.

Ritalin is sold on the street and at schools as a feel-good drug. Since it has a similar high to cocaine or speed, this shouldn't come as a surprise. Ritalin has been linked to violent behavior, according to the International Narcotics Control Board. Some experts believe that the school shootings at Columbine, and other schools, were caused by the Ritalin and other psychotropic drugs reportedly being taken by the children who did the shooting.

Mary Ann Block, DO, P.A., author of *No More Ritalin,* says, "I believe children want to learn and most have the ability to learn. Most of the children I see in my office are very bright. But they often have trouble learning. It is our responsibility as adults and educators to help each child learn the best way she can without giving her stimulants and other types of drugs.

"If a child cannot sit down at a piano and innately know how to play it, we don't call him or her learning disabled and prescribe medications. We teach the child how to play by giving lessons, time to practice, and years to become accomplished. But if that same child cannot immediately learn how to read or write or do math, we call him or her learning disabled."

Bonnie Crammond, Ph.D., a researcher who has studied the similarities between creativity and ADHD behaviors, writes, "Michael Kearney, the youngest college graduate in the world, was diagnosed as a toddler with ADHD and prescribed Ritalin. However, his parents declined drug treatment and decided to nurture Michael's genius with education instead.

"He started school at age three, entered junior college at six, and graduated from the University of South Alabama at ten. His father, Kevin Kearney, refused the notion that Michael's inattention is due to a lack of attention. In fact, children like Michael have an attention surplus. He's so much faster than we are. In two seconds he's figured out what you're going to say. He's toyed with a few answers and now he's looking around waiting for you to finish. It looks like he's not paying attention and it drives teachers crazy."

Indigo Children Speak Out Against Drugs

I asked my Indigo Child, Nicole, to conduct interviews with Indigo Children. I knew that kids would open up to another young person, easier than they would to an adult. My hunch was correct. You'll read the transcripts of these interviews with Indigo Children, and see how they admit their deepest and darkest secrets and feelings to her.

For instance, here is what several Indigo Children had to say about Ritalin, and other psychotropic medication:

Alec: "People should learn how to take care of their problems without a drug or else it will come up some way or another later. When they stop taking the drug, they are not going to know how to deal with the problem that is being suppressed. I know one kid that took Ritalin when he was a kid and now he's a heroin addict.

"People with ADD come up with good ideas and maybe they aren't in the right environment. Or, they need to practice meditating, so that they can build their concentration abilities. Most people with ADD are multi-taskers. Everyone thinks you should stick to one thing but there are some people who can work on a lot of projects and still get them done."

Hunter: "I've known people who have taken Ritalin, and it mellowed them out, but it gave them the chance to get into other, stronger drugs. I think if every kid had someone tell them that they were fine and exactly what they were doing was totally normal and natural, then they'd get through it in their own way it would be a lot easier. Rather than saying that there is a drug that is going to do it."

Dawn: "I think Ritalin is ridiculous. Adults try to put their kids in categories to make themselves feel safe. I've seen it happen a lot of times. Just so they can push it off on something else. 'Oh well, they have ADD, so that's why they're like this.' That's giving an excuse for it. Often times it is misprescribed and it has really messed with a lot of kids. A lot of times Attention Deficit Disorder is from lack of attention from the parent. Not giving the kid attention, I think that is where a lot of the acting out and loud behavior comes from.

"I've seen how Ritalin can make kids become depressed and totally unlike themselves. There have been thousands of cases of suicides on Ritalin. I don't see it as being a positive thing at all. I've heard people say that it's really helped their kid and their kid is doing so much better, but how are they doing better when they are on a drug to make them how the parent wants the kid to be? That is not healthy at all.

"I think parents put their kids on Ritalin because they don't know how to fix the problem with their kids, or they don't want to put in the energy to do so, so they take the easy way out. I think this world is pretty programmed into thinking that prescription pills are the way to fix things."

Elizabeth: "Before a friend of mine began taking Ritalin, he was much more full of life and energy and vibrant. When he was on Ritalin, he was drowsy. He wasn't moody, but he just wasn't in a good mood. He was toned down; his emotions were toned down. When talking to him, he wasn't as present. When he was off of it, he was very interested in things. I think he was so much more himself, much happier, and more beautiful without Ritalin."

Adam: "When I was in third grade, I knew a kid who had ADD or ADHD and he was on Ritalin. He didn't really have any moods when he was on it. He just listened and didn't really talk. I don't think Ritalin should be prescribed because it zones you out and you don't want to do anything. I think drugs are a short term answer to a long term problem."

David: "I've never taken Ritalin, but I have taken Zoloft and Paxil. I got off of Zoloft because it made me sleep too much and I would miss my classes at school. And I got off of Paxil because of night sweats. That stuff is evil. Paxil is supposed to make you less self-conscious and let you go out and be a part of society with less fear and less panic attacks. What it did for me is it got rid of my mental problems, but it gave me different problems that made me even more fearful.

"I think that the only reason that parents put their kids on Ritalin is because they don't want to deal with them. It's like giving a tranquilizer to a horse that's out of control. If you really want the horse to be a good horse, then you have to train it, take care of it, put all of your energy into it, and then it will be a horse that will give back to you. If you just give it tranquilizers, then when it wakes up it's going to be more out of control. I know so many kids that get addicted to other drugs when they're put on Ritalin. If a parent puts their kid on Ritalin, then the parents are just taking an easy way out. There's no excuse. If a kid is hyperactive, then find something for him or her to do, like art or something and they'll probably be calmer after that."

Chris: "I think that in our 'pharmaceutical' society, we have drugs for things like baldness and impotence instead of drugs for serious diseases like malaria. We just try to cure cosmetic things too much. It's the same with the natural medicine thing too, if you have an ailment and then you take a natural pill—but a pill, nonetheless—for it. I don't think that this is the way to solve the problem. Instead of fixing the deep problem, we just coat it over. It's like a breath mint. I think that is a big problem with our society. Instead of fixing the cause, we just try to mask it."

Ryan: "Ritalin is shit, I hate Ritalin. Ritalin got me liking the thought of doing speed. Up to that point I was on Prozac and those kind of drugs, and they didn't work at all. I didn't have any energy and as I think back, well maybe the reason I didn't have any energy was because they were giving me all these drugs I don't need.

"When I got put on Prozac, I had gone to this doctor I had never met and saw him for a half hour and he put me on Prozac and at the time I thought it was kind of cool. That is when it was kind of big and I had just done a report on it and I read how people can not like their personality and take this stuff and it makes them the complete opposite. I thought it was so cool because I wouldn't recognize myself. But I took it and it really make me feel worse. They would tell me, 'you have this thing (depression), but don't worry about it, you're not any different.'

"Telling me I'm not different, but knowing that I had this thing, made me feel I had an excuse to screw off. So, I screwed off, and then they put me on Ritalin. I took the ADD test and I didn't have it. But I seemed a little distracted, I'm not hyperactive, but distracted, so they put me on it and the first day I took it I thought, "whoa, this stuff makes you feel like a spaz.

"I was doing home study at the time and I did a week's homework in one day. My parents thought it was great. But then it goes away and you feel like death, like you're going to kill yourself. So I started taking too much of it and that really screws with your body chemistry. I read that the average animal, after it's heart beats 800 million times, it dies. I was thinking, shit this stuff makes my heart beat 3 times as fast, this must not be too good for me. Speeding up my heart rate. I found out that it was pretty much speed.

"After about a month of doing Ritalin, I was really lethargic and it didn't help me with homework anymore. I pretty much turned into a zombie. Nobody recognized me. I had friends at school that I stopped talking to. I couldn't even stand being myself. After I got off of Ritalin, I started doing speed because I liked the whole feeling. It pisses me off that I was ever given Ritalin because, for what?

"I was fifteen, and you know what? All kids have trouble at fifteen. I think Ritalin is a terrible drug. Kids are thrown on that like antibiotics for a cold. And now, I see kids being put on this shit at age six or seven, or even earlier.

"I think adults give Ritalin to kids because it's an easy way out, an alternative to parenting your kids, and to dealing with the real issue. I think a lot of parents don't really know what Ritalin is and what it does. It's a drug, it gets you high, and then you become addicted. Once your body is addicted to something, it opens that door to addiction. Once you open that door to addiction, it's so hard to get rid of it. It's impossible, it will always be there."

Gabrielle Zale, an art and music therapist who has successfully helped kids with ADHD symptoms through her creativity projects says, "I have seen these children medicated heavily which is just the opposite of what they need. I have also seen these children beg not to be medicated and the system medicated them anyway."

Little Lightworkers

Indigo Children are little lightworkers with nervous systems that are wired for a new world. When they're labeled ADHD, the medical community says that this diagnosis stands for Attention Deficit with Hyperactivity Disorder. However, as a Doctor of Psychology, a former psychotherapist, a parent, and as one who has studied the phenomena, I say that ADHD actually stands for Attention Dialed into a Higher Dimension!

Gifted and ADHD children share many similar characteristics, including high I.Q., creativity, and a penchant for risk-taking. In fact, experts say that the only difference between a gifted child and an ADHD child is that gifted children finish the projects they start, whereas ADHD children leave projects unfinished. Perhaps what ADHD children need, then, is guidance with respect to organizational skills, instead of Ritalin.

"ADD does not produce delinquency," says Jeffrey Freed, M.A.T., author of *Right-Brained Children in a Left-Brained World,* "but I believe the mislabeling and shaming associated with it are contributing factors. The majority of these rebellious misfits might have led happy, productive lives were it not for their 'crime' of having a different learning style."

Many researchers believe that Einstein, Edison, da Vinci, and other great thinkers would have been labeled ADD were they alive today.

Although Indigos learn and act differently, it doesn't mean that they're less intelligent. Dr. Jane Healy, author of *Endangered Minds,* states that I.Q. scores are up among students today, as compared to prior generations of students. These Indigo Children are no dummies! It's just that their overall I.Q. score reflects a shift, with higher scores in nonverbal intelligence ratings, and a dip in the verbal skills department. But, since I.Q. ratings are derived from combining nonverbal and verbal skills, the overall ranking is higher today than ever before.

However, you may not see evidence of the Indigo Children's intelligence in their report card. Instead, their brilliance shines through in high scores on video games, in creating gorgeous beaded necklaces, or memorizing every word to their favorite songs.

A woman named Josie approached me at my workshop with tears in her eyes and her arms outstretched, waiting to embrace me. She exclaimed that after reading my books about working with angels, she'd experienced Divine intervention with her 13-year-old son, Chris.

"Chris was out of control before I began working with his angels," Josie explained to me. "He wouldn't come home on time, and he was using drugs. His schoolwork was a mess. Then my aunt brought home one of your books, and I read how to talk to Chris's angels. I really didn't believe in angels at the time. I thought they were like Santa Claus—a myth. But I was desperate to help my son, so I gave it a try.

"I silently talked to Chris's guardian angels, even though I wasn't really sure I was doing it right. I wasn't even sure that he had angels, the way he was acting like a devil and all! But I saw results almost immediately. I kept talking to those angels every night."

I asked Josie how Chris was doing these days. "

"He's great!" she beamed. "He's happy, off drugs, and he's doing well in school."

Entering Your Children's Dreams

If you're having difficulty talking with your Indigo Children, you can have a heart-to-heart conversation with them in their dreams. There are two ways to do so:

1. Through dream interactions. Before you go to sleep, tell your unconscious mind of your intentions. Say, "Tonight, while I'm dreaming, I intend to enter [children's names] dreams and have an interaction with them. I intend that we will have a healing experience during this dream interaction."

When you wake up, you may not remember the dream, but you'll know that something happened during the night. Your children will have the same sense, and you should see evidence of a healing right away.

2. Talking in their sleep. To engage in this method, you'll have to be awake while your children are dreaming. Wait until you see their eyes moving rapidly, and then you'll know they're dreaming. This may take 20 minutes to one hour after they fall asleep. Or, set your alarm clock to wake up one hour before your children do.

Many Indigo Children are "holographic learners." When someone is talking, the Indigo Child "scans" the other person and receives his or her information, like a computer file being downloaded. The Indigo Child must then wait for the person to stop talking about the information that has already been downloaded and digested.

Indigo Children become bored and restless in classrooms when their teachers lecture about topics that these kids already "get." Sometimes the children just know that the topic is completely irrelevant to their Life Purpose, and to the way that life will be on Earth when they reach adulthood.

Could *you* remain interested in a topic that was completely irrelevant to your life? When we were children, we listened to teachers because we were promised that their lessons would help us "someday." Indigo Children don't have the same sort of blind trust in this promise.

Impulsivity and Intuition

Impulsivity in children is also related to intuition. It's a trait considered a hallmark characteristic of the label "ADD." But what is "impulsivity"? Perhaps it's a precursor to following intuition and inner guidance. Instead of being punished or drugged for this behavior, it's a skill that needs to be fine-tuned and honed.

Sometimes, impulsivity involves the sentiment: "I must have this object now!" That type of impulsivity usually stems from the emptiness of not knowing one's Life Purpose, and trying desperately to stop the existential pain immediately.

Hyperactivity and impulsiveness stem from the little lightworker's sense of time urgency with respect to their Life Purpose. Many adult lightworkers report having a similar feeling, like a chronic tightness in their gut. They feel a strong compulsion to "do something" to make the world a better place. It comes from an inner knowing that your Purpose is needed in the world—now. Although Indigos are still young, with small bodies, their Purposes are crucial to the world. If their Purpose is thwarted or blocked by asking them to perform meaningless tasks, they become frustrated. That is one root of their hyperactivity.

Very often, impulsivity is actually a strong instinctual response that shouldn't be stopped. Is it unhealthy to fidget when you're around a person whom you intuitively feel is dishonest? Many hyperactive and impulsive children are simply responding to overwhelming energies impeding their nervous systems.

I watched two young Indigo boys go through this recently. They were seated at a table in a restaurant with a group of people. The adults were drinking, and had become loud and boisterous. Blaring music bounced off the bare stucco walls. Waiters walked quickly between the tables. The scene was definitely chaotic. The two boys reacted to all of this energy predictably. Unlike the adults, who were sedating themselves with alcohol and food, the boys chose to get up and walk around the restaurant. Their instinct to escape took over! The parents were oblivious to the boys' meandering at first, but as soon as they noticed, they'd yell at the boys to return to the table. I wouldn't want to return to someone who was yelling at me, would you?

Then, I watched in horror as the adults fed the children sugary desserts. I could tell that the children were in for an equally hectic evening. Their sensitive nervous systems would now go off the

Richter scale of hyperactivity, thanks to the sugar.

The Los Angeles school board voted in August 2002 to eliminate all soda pop sales from school campuses during school hours. Any parent can effect the same results by rounding up other parents, and visiting the school board meetings. Present them with statistics and charts, and strongly imply that they won't be re-elected to their school board positions, unless they do something about eliminating soda and junk food from campuses immediately.

Remember that junk food and soda are big moneymakers for schools, so you may need to present creative alternatives for fund-raising.

With visual Indigo Children, use phrases to reflect connecting with the world visually, such as:

- "I see what you mean."
- "Please take a look at this."
- "Can you picture that?"
- "What do you see in your future?"
- "How do you view this situation?"

It's also helpful to draw pictures or write lists for your visually oriented Indigo Children. Teach them to set goals for themselves, and break them down into small steps (such as writing one page of a book report each day). Have them write these goals and steps on a chart, and help them check them off as they complete each step. You'll help them learn how to organize themselves by giving them visual tools.

By speaking your Indigo's language, you can increase the likelihood of clear communication.

Parent-Child Visualization Projects

Help your children make a "dream board," where they cut out magazine pictures of whatever they dream of being, having, or doing. Don't limit or shame the children if they focus on material goals and choose pictures of people with great physiques, or if they cut out pictures of expensive automobiles. This is "basic manifestation," something that they have to start with. They'll soon realize that these objects can *add* to life happiness, but the objects aren't "*IT*." Then, they'll turn to visualizing and manifesting more spiritual ideals.

Have your children visualize and manifest getting *A*'s and awards at school, and it will happen. As a "bedtime story," have your children visualize getting along with the kids and teachers at school, and it will happen. Teach your children to see what they want, not what they don't want.

Aromatherapy

You've probably heard of "aromatherapy," the alternative health practice of using essential oils and flower essences to positively impact health, mood, and energy levels. Well, science is corroborating the powerful effects of smell and aromatherapy. New studies show, for instance, that the scent of lavender has measurable sedative and relaxing effects.

To help your children relax and sleep better, make or purchase a "sleep pillow." Usually, these are made of silk cloth, stuffed with flaxseed, and scented with lavender oil. You can purchase these eye pillows (small, long pillows) or "dream pillows" (available at health-food stores, yoga studios, and metaphysical centers).

However, you can also sprinkle lavender oil (which you can purchase at any health-food store) on your children's pillowcase and sheets and gain similar results. If you can find the oil of valerian root, this has also been found to be an effective sleep agent.

Exercise: Shifting Brain Chemistry and Behavior Naturally

What if the world of science discovered a pill that could instantly alleviate depression and anxiety, and also help a person lose weight, live longer, and feel happier? And what if this pill was freely available to everyone, without a doctor's prescription, and at a relatively low cost? All the newspapers would herald this remarkable discovery. People would clamor to buy the pill!

Well, such a cure-all does exist, and its effectiveness is backed up by countless scientific studies (many of them are listed in the bibliography of this book). Its called "exercise." Studies show that aerobic exercise in particular—running, jogging, stair climbing, swimming, bicycling, and brisk walking—increases the production of the brain chemical *serotonin* and other feel-good neurotransmitters.

Several ADD and ADHD experts have stated, "If children would jog once or twice a day, we could virtually eliminate the need for Ritalin prescriptions." Yet, because no pharmaceutical company profits from exercising, physical fitness isn't pushed as vehemently as stimulants.

Making Exercise Fun

Most likely, your children associate exercise with their physical education (P.E.) classes at school. Since Indigo Children tend to be shy, sensitive, or even socially phobic, P.E. is often an excruciating experience. Coaches force them to run and kids tease or bully them. No wonder they relate exercising to emotional pain!

To help your kids overcome these feelings, choose a fun workout such as renting a bicycle-built-for-two, rowing boats together, or going on a family hike. Suggest that your children listen to music while exercising. At least two major studies have found that listening to any form of music while exercising reduces the feeling of drudgery associated with the activity and makes time seem to pass faster.

A new study shows that just 10 minutes of cardio-vascular activity has an observable positive effect on elevating mood and energy!

I normally run outside, which is a great idea for Indigo Children, since studies show that sunshine and fresh air stimulates production of the feel-good brain chemicals, especially serotonin. Since cardiovascular exercise already promotes serotonin, exercising outside is like getting a double dosage. However, during inclement weather, I'll run on a treadmill. During those times, I love to watch music videos to entertain and inspire me.

Here are some additional ways to motivate your children to adopt an exercise program:

- Buy your kids a subscription to an inspirational monthly magazine about exercise, such as *Runner's World, Shape, Fitness, Men's Fitness,* or *Yoga Journal.*
- Invest in a good pair of shoes that are appropriate for your children's exercise choice, as well as heavy running socks.
- Many cities have stores that sell used sporting equipment, such as bicycles and treadmills, at bargain prices. You can find these stores in the telephone directory, listed under "sporting goods."
- Attend or watch on television, sporting events such as track meets, basketball games, or tennis matches with your kids to stimulate their interest in sports.
- Offer your children incentives for exercising, such as a small amount of money, or a new CD from the music store. It's important that you compliment them on their efforts, too.
- If your Indigo Child is a teenager or older, invest in a family membership to a gym or health club. You'll get to spend more time together, and also have the opportunity to work out in close proximity to each other.
- Probably the most valuable contribution you could give your children is to exercise yourself.

Whether you know it or not, your children watch and react to whatever you do. Sometimes, your children counter-reacts (does the opposite); and other times, your children mimic you. My parents are avid exercisers, and they definitely inspired me to adopt a healthful lifestyle. Find out what time of day your energy levels are at their highest, and work out during that time of the day.

Hypoglycemic or ADHD?

"Low blood sugar, or hypoglycemia, is the most significant underlying problem I find in children who exhibit behavioral problems," says Mary Ann Block, D.O., P.A., the author of *No More Ritalin.* She lists the behavioral symptoms of hypoglycemia as "the child who is agitated or irritable when he or she wakes up in the morning, or before meals, and then is better after eating; and the child with the Jekyll and Hyde behavior, who is sweet and fine one minute, and then for no apparent reason, is agitated, angry, and irritable the next."

Dr. Block says, "The treatment for hypoglycemia is simple: Change the child's diet. Make sure that the child never gets hungry, and eliminate refined carbohydrates, such as candy, cakes, pies, and soft drinks from [their] diet."

My Indigo son, Chuck, experiences hypoglycemia when he goes too long without eating. On his own, Chuck has discovered how to keep his blood sugar high by eating frequent, small, and healthful snacks. He avoids caffeine, chocolate, and sugar. When his blood sugar drops, Chuck becomes tired and irritable. But he recognizes that his low mood and energy is temporary and food-related, so he doesn't buy into it. He simply takes it as a signal to eat. Once Chuck eats, his energy level and mood return to their normal state very quickly.

I agree with Dr. Block's advice about making sure that your hypoglycemic-prone children don't become hungry, even if it seems inconvenient. She writes:

"It is best that the child with the symptoms of hypoglycemia go no longer than two hours without eating. If your child has this problem and tells you she is hungry, but dinner will be ready in thirty minutes, it is tempting to have her wait for dinner. I strongly suggest that you find something for your child to eat right then. Don't make her wait for dinner. When children with hypoglycemia get hungry, they need to eat now!"

Dr. Block suggests giving children a small snack of trail mix, nuts, or a peanut butter sandwich, which will quickly stabilize their blood sugar without ruining their appetite for dinner.

Supplements and ADHD Behavior

Researcher Stephen Schoenthaler, who has studied inmate, juvenile delinquent, and school populations extensively, found that children's I.Q. rises, and their delinquent behavior significantly drops, after they take vitamin and mineral supplements. Another researcher, Dr. Richard Carlton, found that vitamin and mineral supplements lead to significant improvements in academics and behavior.

Carlton reported, "Some children gained three to five years in reading comprehension within the first year of treatment, and all children in special education classes became mainstreamed, and their grades rose significantly." When some of the students whom Carlton was studying stopped taking vitamins and minerals, there was an immediate decline in their grades. Carlton also noted that the students taking vitamin and mineral supplements became more sociable and exhibited better moods.

The supplement ingredients that helped students the most were magnesium, vitamin B-6, vitamin C, thiamine, folic acid, and zinc. It was found that *manganese* (not to be confused with *magnesium*) caused irritability and difficulty concentrating in some students, so the researchers removed it from the study.

Children who are hyperactive have lower serotonin levels than children who aren't hyperactive, according to a study published in the *Pediatrics Journal.* Low serotonin can result in lethargy, depression, and food cravings. When the researchers gave hyperactive children some vitamin B-6, their serotonin levels significantly increased. Another study compared the serotonin levels for children who received vitamin B-6 with another group of children who received Ritalin. Only the B-6 group showed elevated serotonin levels, and these positive results lasted long after the group stopped receiving B-6.

Children who received magnesium supplements showed a significant decrease in hyperactivity, compared to control groups who received placebos in a study of children ages 7 through 12. Since colas and many processed foods contain phosphoric acid, which leaches magnesium from the body, it's essential that you read food labels and steer clear of phosphoric acid.

One study found that 95 percent of ADHD children were deficient in magnesium. Another found that not only did ADHD children lack sufficient magnesium levels, but they were also deficient in iron, copper, and calcium. The researchers concluded, "It is necessary to supplement trace elements in children with hyperactivity." In other words, we must make sure that children who are hyperactive get daily vitamin and mineral supplements that contain magnesium, iron, copper, and calcium.

Fatty Acids and Behavior

Many new studies show that children labeled ADHD also have essential fatty acid deficiencies. You've probably seen bottles of "flaxseed oil" in the refrigerators at health-food stores, and may have wondered what they were for. Well, many people are supplementing their diets with one capful of flaxseed oil daily. This is an easy way to ensure that you have a sufficient amount of essential fatty acids.

Symptoms of essential fatty-acid deficiencies include excessive thirst, frequent urination, dry patches of skin, and miniature whiteheads on the backs of the arms. One study found that 40 percent of boys with ADHD symptoms also had these symptoms. Some experts believe that ADHD behavior is a symptom of essential fatty-acid deficiency.

It's so easy to correct this deficiency! Simply purchase flaxseed oil, hempseed oil, or soy oil. Pour one teaspoon daily in your children's salad, smoothie, or other foods. And while you're at it, make sure that you put a teaspoon in your own meals. Your hair and skin will shine with new luster, making it definitely worth the extra calories and fat grams!

Food Dye, Sugar, Preservatives, and Additives

Food dye, sugar, and preservatives have been scientifically linked to ADHD and ADD behaviors. At least 17 studies have linked food dye with hyperactivity and insomnia, especially in young children. In one study, 150 of 200 children (75 percent) slept better and were less irritable and restless after synthetic food coloring was removed from their diet. Another study showed that children had improved behavior after changing to a food-dye free diet, and that the improvement was long lasting.

Yale University researchers gave refined white sugar to children and compared their blood adrenaline levels before and after sugar consumption. They discovered that the amount of adrenaline soared ten times higher following consumption of the sugar! Adrenaline, as you know, is the heart-pumping chemical that prepares you for combat or dangerous situations. When schools in New York banned food dyes and additives from school lunches, they experienced the most dramatic rise in academic performance for any school district ever recorded.

Two studies of imprisoned violent and aggressive young people showed a dramatic (47 to 77 percent) drop in the number of aggressive and criminal acts, as well as suicide attempts, when sugar and food additives were removed from the inmates' meals.

It's not okay to rationalize, "Well, a little bit of food dye won't hurt my children." One study examined the hyperactivity of children after they ate just one cookie containing food dye. Within one hour of eating the one cookie, the children showed increased hyperactivity. Another study found decreased performance in hyperactive students within hours of ingesting food dye.

Indigo Children, gifted children, children who are labeled ADD or ADHD, and adult lightworkers are almost always right-brain dominant. Scientific studies on the blood flow and activity of ADHD children's brains find that they use their visual center of the brain more than their logic-center lobe.

This means that they interact with the world primarily with the right hemisphere of their brain, which focuses upon visions and feelings and relates to nonverbal studies such as art, music, math, philosophy, psychology, and psychic arts. Right brain-dominant people can make excellent writers and speakers, provided they learn how to translate their mental pictures and strong internal feelings into words.

The left hemisphere, in contrast, is more concerned with words, and the left-brained person will be naturally proficient with grammar and vocabulary. The left-brained person is usually orderly and follows authority without question (and even welcomes it!).

The right-brained person is intuitive, only following "benevolent authority"—and then, only when they understand and trust the authority figure's motivation and goals. They learn by seeing, and do better with charts, graphs, slides, and demonstrations than by reading or listening to a lecture.

Because right-brained people have such acute senses, they're easily distracted. They can hear every little click of the school clock's hand, and the high-pitch sound of the fluorescent lighting.

Hungry for Creativity

Indigo Children need outlets to express their powerful energy. Exercise is one way to let the steam out so they don't explode like a pressure cooker. And creativity is another important means. In many of my sessions, the angels come through and suggest that Indigo Children get involved in some sort of creative venture. Any form will do: making beaded jewelry, decorating a bedroom, photography, dance, music, building sandcastles, doodling, or creative cooking.

Researcher Bonnie Cramond found scientific research that showed that both groups (highly creative and ADHD) are:

- prone to engage in disruptive, attention-seeking behavior in the classroom.
- not valued by teachers as much as children who are more conforming.

• apt to engage in thrill-seeking or sensation-seeking behaviors. Researchers believe that sensation seeking may lead a creative person to discover new experiences, which they incorporate into their ideas and inventions. In addition, risk-taking (similar to sensation seeking) is correlated with business and financial success. This trait may also explain why Indigo Children become easily bored once they "get" what someone is teaching them.

• likely to be "inattentive." They daydream, think of new ideas, and pay attention to inner guidance and spiritual guidance, and tune out conversations or activities that don't ring true or fit with their passion.

• known to exhibit high levels of "overexciteability," or a tendency to fidget and be hyperactive.

• often passionate and have outbursts of temper.

• frequently socially awkward. They may be shy, defensive, or aloof because they feel different than others, and it's easier to be alone than suffer ridicule.

Dr. Cramond concluded, "Perhaps what differentiates individuals who use their rapid ideation to create versus those who are disruptive and unproductive is the talent and *opportunity* to express their energies and ideas in some creative mode." So, giving your Indigo Children creative outlets and giving them support for their "differentness" is essential.

Doreen Virtue, Ph.D. holds three degrees in Counseling Psychology, and is the former director of a teenage alcohol and drug abuse unit. She is the mother of two sons and two stepdaughters. Doreen has interviewed Indigo Children and their parents around the world. She authored chapters for the book, "The Indigo Children" by Lee Carroll and is the author of "The Care and Feeding of Indigo Children" and "The Crystal Children." Her other books include "Healing with the Angels" and "Angel Therapy." For more information on Doreen's books, oracle cards, and workshops, please visit her web site at >www.AngelTherapy.com<.

19.

Think about the title of this book for a moment:
"Raising Psychic Children."
Try to think about this in a different way.
"Raising" as to "lift up."
To Lift your Child Up.
When you think about it like this
Then it offers a whole new understanding.

You are here to lift your child toward Heaven.
The rest will happen on its own.
You must learn how to surrender your child to God.

20.

Don't listen to what the "authorities" tell you about
Raising a Psychic Child.
You will ultimately have to discard what I say as well.
Listen to your heart.
It already knows what needs to happen.
Just try to get out of your head.
Get out of your own way
And let it happen by itself.

The less you direct it,
The more it will direct you.

21.

The children are here to mirror a New World.
They do that by accessing a web of consciousness
Where they can work as One Mind.
It doesn't matter how it happens.
The details can't be understood with the mind.
All that counts is that you realize that you are not
Separate from that web.
They are calling you to be part of this Great Work.
But the children need you to help them.
That is the whole purpose of this book.

How can you best help your children access their gifts?
By listening to them.

22.

Listen between the lines.
They have so much to say,
But their minds don't work the same as yours.
They haven't been pushed entirely into a linear pattern
That makes it hard to wind like a circle
Around what they know and need to express.
But in the center of this circle is an answer that the world needs.

Look to the center in everything they say.
Don't expect them to speak to you as you speak to them.
It would be better to turn the table on this
And enter the circle yourself.
Then you'll understand in a way you couldn't before.

23.

If you learn how to really listen to us,
Then it will help you in ways you may not expect.
The listening will be the gift.
Hearing will follow.
Understanding will be the result.

When you understand what the children are trying to say,
Then you will be able to speak their language
And live as they live.
We're not asking you to give us anything,
But to accept more of who you are.

There is a Psychic Child within you right now,
And it has so much it wants to say.
Listen to us,
And you will learn to hear yourself.

24.

Try to remember that looking and seeing
Are two different things.
So are listening and hearing.
You can look at something but never really see it.
Likewise,
You can listen to someone but never really hear him.

Your children long to be seen,
And yearn to be heard.
It is the first gift you can give.
Listen with your heart,
And see with your soul.
If you are able to give them this gift,
Then you will be helping them in ways you cannot imagine.

Then they will help you remember who you are.

The following article is excerpted from
Children of the New World.

Who Are These Children?

by Barbara Meister Vitale

It was a beautiful, sparkling spring day. As children sometimes do, I was lying on my back in a field of wildflowers watching the clouds and thinking. Thinking about how lonely I felt, how different I felt, how all the sounds, colors, and beings I saw made me feel overwhelmed. I remember just wanting to feel like the seven-year-old that I was.

At this time in our dream there are many special children choosing to come to Earth. Like me, some are feeling alone, different, and even frightened. Some of them remember why they have come—others don't. They are all asking for help to survive.

Who are these children?

They have been labeled just about everything. Those in the establishment have given them labels like: ADD (attention deficit disorder), LD (learning disabled), BD (behavioral disorder), and psychotic. Parents and those who are reaching for a more spiritual explanation are passing out labels such as: Indigo, Masters, or Children of the Light. These children are surprising us with their deep, spiritual understanding of the worlds around them and why they have come here. Although they are enlightened and have come to teach us love and peace, the bottom line is, they are still children sometimes wanting to be treated as children.

When they say they want to be treated like children, they are not talking about the old traditional beliefs such as: spare the rod, spoil the child; children should be neither seen nor heard; or children have empty brains that must be filled by the adults around them. They want to be treated as the souls they are. At the same time they do not want to be worshipped. As I have talked to the parents of these children I have found some actually being afraid of their children, while others think their children can do no wrong. I was talking to a parent at a camp for the children. This parent said, "I don't want my child attending any of the meetings, he knows everything already." Another commented, "Don't tell my daughter 'no.'" These children were totally unguided and disrespectful of others feelings. When I asked the teenagers what they felt was the most helpful to them, they answered, "Discipline based on consequences. We will remember the rest."

These children have a core understanding of who they really are. I asked a thirteen-year-old, "Why did you come to Earth?" Coming from someone so young, his answer stunned me. He very quietly spoke, "I came here to become more enlightened, to help God express itself. I want more practice in applying the Universal Laws by expressing Love and Peace." Wow! Then I asked, "What do you want to be when you grow up?"

He gave a sigh like how could she ask this question, but he answered, "It really doesn't matter. I live in the moment. The important thing to do is to remember and follow my Soul's path." At this point I just stopped asking questions.

So how can we help? Remember they are children. They enjoy playing and having friends their own age. This may take some doing. Many of these children do not relate to children at school or in their own neighborhoods. Finding them places, such as camps, where they can be together with other children who also remember, is important. One child at such a gathering told me, "I feel like I am no longer alone." Another said, "I don't feel weird anymore." It is important that they see everyone as special and remember that some people just haven't remembered that they are really special. I remember my grandmother saying, "God doesn't make mistakes."

With all of their spiritual awareness, the children often have difficulty applying it to real life. Although they feel equal to everyone on Earth, it is helpful for them to understand that the experience of living on this planet helps makes it easier to apply spiritual principles. Because they have had this experience, parents, grandparents, and others may have knowledge that could help them personally. We can reach out by sharing through stories and our own experiences. The children can listen and discriminate what is useful for their own soul's path.

Since these children are very powerful, it is important to show them what the responsibility of carrying this power looks like. Guide them to watch and notice how people's actions affect each other. Demonstrate how everything we do has a consequence. Activities that reflect the following can be done through play or scientific exploration: if you don't water a flower it will die; being angry can effect your health; love creates positive consequences; or, on this planet every thought you have creates your reality. These are just a few of the many spiritual concepts to be explored. Ask the children for ideas. Their job is to decide if the thoughts and emotions they are having are creating the life and results they want. If their thoughts aren't creating the life they want, then help them find ways to change them.

I remember one of my spiritual teachers took me out on a small hill. It was a beautiful sunny day with large fluffy clouds. We began to talk about how beautiful it was. Suddenly he said something very hurtful to me, and I began to feel very sad. The sky darkened and it began to rain. He then apologized and told me how proud he was of me. The clouds disappeared and the sun came out. What a lesson. I realized that not only did my thoughts change my perception of the weather, but that I had allowed his words to change me. I also realized that everything I said and every thought I had, had the potential of affecting everything.

When I was in England, I met a mother who told me the following story. She said, "I told my three-year-old son that it was time for him to start school. He looked at me very calmly and announced, "I don't need to go to school. I remember everything from before. Besides, wherever I go I leave a pair of my eyes behind and they send me back any information I need to know." This child understood that nothing is learned, but everything is remembered.

For these children, surviving the present educational system can be a little tough. They often have a very different learning style. They process ideas and concepts on a multidimensional level. What does that mean? They often prefer doing several tasks at once, jumping from one to the other, and dreaming the answer before they know the process. This allows them to cross reference memories. One brush stoke made while creating a picture may give them the solution to a chemistry problem. Many of the great scientists such as Nikola Tesla, Buckminster Fuller, George Washington Carver, and Albert Einstein dreamed or got their ideas while gazing at clouds. They would sometimes pull information from the past or future. Don't be surprised if the children do the same!

Although very intelligent, I have met several children reading below grade level or failing math. I was asked to spend time with a beautiful young man who was having trouble in school. Basically he couldn't read. The letters and words made no sense to him. As we began to talk, he began to explain quantum astronomy as it applied to our galaxy and beyond. An idea struck me, if he could think in such abstract mathematical symbols, what would happen if he could apply those to the letters on the page? I asked him to give each word or letter one of the symbols he was seeing in his head. Within a few minutes he was reading above grade level. The secret is finding the key within their individual universal memories.

Color psychology is everywhere. It is talked about in healing, marketing, and nutrition. For those of you who can see colors around a person, you know there is a color ray that comes down through the top of the head. This color connects the higher self or soul of a person to their physical body. Using this color to center the children often works. They can visualize their magic color, wear it, see themselves in a bubble of color, use a colored light bulb, wear colored glasses, write with color, or use plastic sheets of it to put over reading. Usually the color that works for the child is their favorite color. Ask them which colors make them feel safe, smart, strong, loved, peaceful, or make the words look larger.

Once the child has found the information in memory, it is important to ground it to this world. The most effective way to do this is through movement. The movement can be directly connected to the information, such as writing words in the air or painting, or it can be just movement for the joy of moving, such as creative dancing. A fun activity is to ask the children to dance what they think Peace would feel like. The first time I saw this I sat and cried with joy.

Sound and energy are all around us. They are a part of our dimensional reality. Being aware of these along with color is being aware of a part of ourselves. Since ancient times music has been used to heal and change our moods. Recently scientists have discovered that the vibrations of a cat's purr may be able to help heal broken bones, and relieve pain. The vibrations of a dolphin's sonar, has a profound effect on children who are considered autistic. The Bulgarian, Georgi Lozanov explored the fact that baroque music, deep breathing, and visualization balanced the body and brain, increasing the capacity for learning. I also believe it brings the heart into play. Encourage the children to experiment with color, sound, smell, and energy to discover how it is affecting them and how they can use it to create.

These children are likely to tell teachers and parents they are wrong. This is not always a good idea for survival. Help the children develop the skills of communicating without making the other person feel wrong, especially adults. The following words and phrases are empowering for both the child and the adult: help me understand; what if; is it possible; or is this true under all circumstances? Help them develop a sense of when it is important to speak and when it is OK to just be silent. Remind them that there are several different realities in this universe with different beliefs of the meaning of truth. We each can choose which reality to create out of a universe of unlimited possibilities.

Listen to the children! When asked what they wanted the most, it was to be heard. Although they can be exasperating at times, they do have important information to share. If they tell you they have seen an angel, talked to a tree, or played with a special being, please acknowledge the information. Listen rather than say, "Oh, that's just your imagination." When they have frightening nightmares, teach them how to make them go away and how to protect themselves. If they share scientific information, check it out together. Whatever you do, remember what the children share is their truth. Who's to say it isn't the truth. They have a lot to say that will help us move to the new world.

One of the children said, "Your eyes tell me who you are but your heart tells me if you remember who you are."

One afternoon a friend of mine watched a lovely little girl running gaily around the yard gathering fall leaves and putting them in a basket. "What have you gathered?" Susan asked. "Tree stars!" was the little girl's reply. "Tree stars?" Susan asked in amazement. The girl answered, "Yes, when God is done with the stars they come here and pretend to be leaves. They turn color and fall off, then you can pick them up and carry them home."

I have been picking up baskets of tree stars ever since and have found that each one is full of God!

Do lots of pretending. Try not to impose your belief system. So far our beliefs haven't worked very well. Remind them of the dream and that everything is pretending. The secret is to watch what you pretend.

Pretend Love, Joy, and Peace for that is what we are.

Barbara Meister Vitale is the Director of the Meta-Intelligence Institute, and author of "Unicorns are Real" and "Free Flight." She is completing the book, "Children of the New Worlds." Although intuitive and creative, Barbara did not learn to read until she was 12 years old. Since that time she has earned masters and specialist degrees in Early Childhood, Learning Disabilities, and Administration. In 1980 the Lakota people adopted her. Several spiritual elders in traditions, ceremonies, and star knowledge have trained her. As an international speaker, she gives a unique perspective to life and learning.

25.

A Light has come into the world that your mind cannot
understand.
You have been waiting for this for a very long time.
Your children can see this light,
But you may not.
And yet it is just as real inside you as it is in them.
Look into their eyes and you will begin to understand.
Then look into your own eyes.
You will see that there is no difference.

Look into a baby's eyes and you will perceive something
That transcends the intellect.
She won't look away,
But will stare and smile and love you.
You will walk away feeling different than before.
Your heart will feel lighter,
And your mind will be clear.

The next time someone looks at you,
Don't look away.
Take a risk and hold the gaze as long as you can.
A wall may fall down.
A damn may break,
All because you had the courage to See.

26.

Do you want to know the best way to raise your children
So they will be able to awaken their psychic gifts?
Here is the best advice I can give:
See them!
Really See them!

And then listen to them.

27.

The children who are coming into the world today
Aren't able to fit into the boxes you built for them.
You may place a box in front of them,
And they will sit beside it.
Don't expect anything less than this.
If they sat inside the box
Then you wouldn't learn anything from them.

28.

The New Children know that their psychic gifts mean
nothing
Without the source that gives them life.
They may do things that you think are unbelievable,
Or say things that are beyond their years,
And then they will turn around and be an ordinary child
again.
But at the center of it all
Is the foundation that makes it all possible.
Love!

When your heart is open,
Miracles happen by themselves.
Your children understand this.
When love is the center of your life,
Then your mind expands to include
A universe of possibilities.
Your children understand this as well.

Don't try to teach your children how to be psychic.
Let them teach you about love,
Then they will understand who they are.

29.

Your children can teach you how unnecessary words are.
If you listen to their words you may become confused.
But if you watch them with an open heart,
Then everything will make sense.

You thought this book would be about raising a Psychic Child.
It is really the opposite.
Ultimately,
It's about allowing a Psychic Child to raise you.

30.

Here is another way to understand this.
Approach the situation as if you and your child
Are new to the world.
You may know more than he does in some ways,
But he is closer to eternity than you.
His mind is more open than yours.
He doesn't make as many assumptions.
The truth is that you are both new to this planet,
Because it is being recreated every moment.
You are being recreated every moment as well.
Hold his hand and walk with amazed eyes,
And you will learn together.

Look at everything as if you've never seen it before.

31.

When you were young
There was a thin veil that separated you from
What you saw with your eyes
And what you saw in your imagination.
That veil grew thicker as you became older,
Partly because adults told you that one was real
And the other was an illusion.

Don't treat your own children in this way.

They see things that you cannot understand with your mind.
There is ultimately no difference between the physical world
And the world you see when you close your eyes.
Neither is real.
The children already know this
So they are able to play between these two worlds.
That is where the Gift is found.

You, too, can find this place,
But only if you stop looking.

32.

Your child's wisdom will bloom and flower
In many different ways.
Be open to every one of them,
Though you may not understand with your mind.
Understanding is a gift you will receive once you believe.
Believing is like seeing.
Something may be right in front of you
But you may never see it.
Likewise,
A truth could be with you this very moment,
But unless you believe it is there
You will never realize the gifts it could offer.

Don't forget that your child chose you for important reasons.
You have so much to offer her,
And she will return with gifts of her own.
You are waking up from a dream together.
What difference does it make who stretches first?

33.

If you allow yourself to be a good learner,
Then you will be a better teacher.
Your children need you to be both.

Learning and teaching are the same thing.
Children ask questions because they want to understand.
But they already Know.
Do you understand the difference?

You are not so different from your child.
Your body may be older,
And you may have more information in your brain.
But information will not help you.
Neither will having an older body.
Your children are closer to this reality
Because their minds are empty
And open to be filled.
Is yours?

Your concepts cannot help you now.
Give them all up
Once and for all.

From A Young Adult Psychic

by Nasata La

All children, all beings are psychic. Everyone has some special, unique ability—all ages, sexes, and races, from all countries and walks of life. Certainly, not everyone can move things with their mind, see and talk with Angels, or recall past lives with perfect clarity, but everyone has some ability that is specific to their life plan and purpose. We are all psychic. For many of us, our abilities lay dormant waiting to be activated, and for others of us our abilities have never been shut down. Many of the children coming in now are awake and aware of their abilities and purpose, not hidden by any veils or social programming. This presents an interesting challenge as to where the child fits into a world that is just now beginning to open up to what is such a clear and natural way of being for the child. Until now, there really hasn't been a place for them in society or even in their own families. We are finally becoming aware enough to recognize and support these children instead of mislabeling and mistreating them. Names like Indigo, Psychic, Crystal, and Special children have been created to describe them more accurately, and parents all around the world have started learning more about who their children really are.

Many people have talked about how it is more difficult to raise an Indigo or Psychic child. There have been books written and support groups formed to help parents find solutions to many of their troubles. A lot of the focus so far has been on how to help the children come to our level in some way, either emotionally, spiritually, physically, or in society. What we perceive as problems, are just the children's reactions to us trying to change them. When we are able to fully support their experience of their purpose for being here, a flow and communion is established. When we find ways to go to their level, the problems do not exist. The whole reason why many of these beings have come is to *raise our vibration*, not for us to lower theirs. They are here to teach us, lead the way, and shake up what has been stuck for a very long time. The world is changing into this new, amazing place where Love is present in everything and everyone, and it is these new children who know it with their whole being, as well as how to get us there.

There is no difference in how you treat a "normal" child and a "psychic" child because they are not different. We all come from the same source of light and are here to have a diversity of experience. What one child can do and another can't has nothing to do with how they should be treated. There is no doubt that raising children is one of the most challenging jobs. Now, here we are in these new times with a whole new set of rules to learn, and there really is no guidebook that covers all of it. LOVE IS THE ANSWER!

LOVE

At the core of every child, adult, animal, plant—every living thing—is the desire to be loved and to Be Love. Love is the most important ingredient of every action, motivation, intent, every single moment. When in doubt ... Love. Love your children. Love each other. Love yourself. There are those who have asked, "Well, what is love anyway?" and rightfully so, for love is not something that many people truly KNOW yet. Love is not only a feeling in your heart, but also a Knowing in your whole being. You cannot get to love by following instructions or imitating someone else's experience of love. Love is an experience that is personal and unique and then you find that it is a union with everyone and everything. Love cannot be thought. The concept of Love can, but the actual state of Love cannot. The minute you "think" you know what Love is, you have put it into a box that it does not fit into. Love is Infinite. I cannot tell you what Love is because it is not a thing, it is who you are.

So, to truly love your children, you must be all of who you are.

This is an exciting challenge because it requires a vividly honest look at what may be standing in the way. Then, there is a letting go, jumping into the unknown. And finally, the process of stepping up to what is known ... your purpose. Once you have reached this place of clear Self, you can focus on expanding and amplifying the quality and quantity of love within you and in your expression. From this space you can fully love your child with clean energy, honest intention, and an open heart. You will be on the same page, coming from the same place, and in a sweet communion.

PATIENCE

An essential part of being a parent, or anyone who is connected with children, is patience. Children and adults are not in the same world. Their maturity, process, and experience are miles apart. What a child understands about things is very different from an adult. Be patient with each other. You are both in the perfect place for you and doing the best that you can.

Many of the new children are not only on a different level from their parents but they are also really in a different world. Some are multi-functioning in many worlds at one time, and this requires a special kind of patience. Your child may be experiencing things that you have no idea about and they may not be able to explain it or tell you about it until they understand it better.

As a child, I distinctly recall being in a room full of beings who were all talking to me at once. Some of them spoke different languages and did not seem to be as aware of each other as they were of me. They were all in vivid color and had clear, loud voices, except for one woman who seemed to be like a dream or an illusion. This woman was my mother. She was trying to tell me to do something and was getting very frustrated because I was not listening to her. In that moment I did not recognize her as real compared to everyone else in the room, whom she did not see at all. I had to practice to even be able to hear my parents at times.

A lot of the new children have lessons to learn that none of us can teach them. Many of them come in already knowing so much more than we do that they do not have anyone from this place to relate to as a teacher in certain areas. So, they are learning their own lessons as they go and may get impatient with the process if it is not fast enough. As a parent, the best thing to do is to be able to recognize those times and be as loving and supportive as possible without trying to fix it. Being patient with your process as well as theirs is a valuable part of having a harmonious family. Your child will see a good example of patience by watching your behavior and learn to adjust in time.

COMMUNICATION

Children thrive on attention from their parents. Being listened to and heard is vital to the development of their self-esteem and positive expression. There are many ways to listen and pay attention to a child. They speak with words but more often they communicate with body language, eyes, facial expression, actions, sounds, movement, attitude, artwork, the way they play, how much they participate, or not. When you learn to communicate with your child with more than just words, a whole vast world opens up with endless opportunities for connection, support, and love. Be interested genuinely in what they say and do. Be alert. Pay attention. Talk to them as an equal. Remember, they are not so much of a child as a big being in a little person's body. Take interest in what matters to them. Get to know each other. Find out what their purpose is and do your best to support and provide for them. Listen carefully for the divine messages that pour forth from their body, mind, and heart. They are our teachers.

RESPECT

When children are treated with respect they learn how to respect others. Respect is the honoring of someone as an equal with an open heart saying, "You are important and valued," with words, actions, and energy. Start from the very beginning of their life by honoring them as much as they deserve. When someone feels acknowledged, that they are important and valid, seen and heard, they have no reason to act out in order to get attention or prove who they are. Respect is key. Even when you may not know what your child is going through, why they are acting a certain way, what they are experiencing, or what on earth they are talking about, always treat them with respect. Chances are they are not talking about anything "on earth" anyway.

BOUNDARIES

Some parents have an overabundance of rules and restrictions while others let their children do anything they want in the name of a happy childhood. It is very important to have clear, recognizable, firm boundaries with children as well as a gentle allowance and freedom to learn by experience. Children who feel caged will lash out, while children who are given anything they want will learn to manipulate and become lazy and rude. When a child is given clear boundaries that are reinforced with consistency and loving guidance, they are able to feel secure in their actions and not have to constantly test limits because of being unsure. Have boundaries with them as you would with any other person. When everyone in the house knows where they stand, valuable energy can be spent on things like love and creativity instead of discipline.

SENSITIVITY

One of the things that all children have in common is sensitivity. Children are OPEN. They are open in more ways than most people know. They take in everything. As adults we have learned to guard ourselves, censor things, and shut out unwanted energy. Children do not have that skill yet. What we take for granted as simple and no big deal, may be major and life changing to a child. Being aware of this will help you understand your children and possibly help them.

Many of the new children have extremely high sensitivities to things like light, dark, color, sound, food, chemicals, pollution, emotions, textures, etc. There are as many different reactions to different things as there are children to have them. These high sensitivities are partly due to their vibration not matching the density of this world and partly due to not being able to fully integrate the different levels of dimension that they are in simultaneously. One of the most common reactions is an allergy to anything not natural or organic, such as soaps, chemicals, plastics, air pollution, synthetic material, the list is very long. Man-made chemicals and products tend to be of a very low vibration and are on their way out. Their molecular structure is becoming unstable as the illusion changes and the higher frequencies are out of phase with them. The easiest way to assist your child's life in being smoother is to do everything organic, including clothing, and limit or eliminate harmful chemicals, cleaners, plastics, and body products.

Another strong sensitivity is to thoughts and emotions. Staying in your center as much as possible will keep you clear and your child clear. Whether it is spoken or not, your child is psychically bonded to you and you to them. You are part of the same Self, and what each of you think and feel, directly affects the other.

DIMENSIONS

Not all of us are in the same dimension at the same time, so what is real for you may or may not be real for your child. There are layers of each dimension as well, called overtones. Also, some of us are not only in one dimension but also in many places at once, multi-tasking. If you're having a hard time understanding where your child is at or what she is talking about, chances are she is somewhere in an overtone of the fourth dimension. Imagine what it would be like to be a child in the fourth dimension while her parents are in the third. What would she need from them? How could they support her in her growth that is not even a part of their reality? Compassion, Patience, Love, Understanding, Unconditional Support, an Openness to learn and let go—these are all things that a parent can give. Learning to think fourth-dimensionally will help you relate to your child. Seeing time as a sphere, honoring Love as your thriving force, being devoted to expansiveness, listening intently to your intuition as it becomes a strong clear voice, letting go of all blocks and negativity, allowing the mind to relax into its full usefulness in perfect balance with your heart—these things will give you easier access to the higher vibrations.

LOVE

Love is the magical presence uniting all of our paths in one big purpose. We are all connected to each other, all special in our own way, and all an integral part of this New World that we are creating together. The time to step into the Light of Love is now. The time to be all of who we truly are is now. Joining hearts as Emissaries of Love we complete the circle around this beautiful planet that is our home and look forward excitedly to the shift into BLISS.

Nasata La is in her early twenties and remembers what it was like to be a Psychic Child. She lives in Ashland, Oregon and began volunteering at James Twyman's office when they started working with the children. Her influence has been invaluable.

34.

When you were young you were trying to find your way
Through the world.
Everything presented a challenge.
Your children are trying to find their way through two
worlds.
This presents challenges you are unable to understand.

Their confusion comes from remembering the unseen world,
While trying to reconcile it with the physical universe.
Don't try to force this.
Allow them to work with their environment
And find their way into balance.

35.

No book will teach you how to raise a Psychic Child.
Your heart is the only true guide.
Keep it open at all times.
Your heart is a remarkable teacher
And it will guide you into worlds
You haven't considered with your mind.
It perceives the deeper rhythms
That connect the two worlds.
It does not teach with information,
But by experiencing Compassion and Understanding.
If you listen to the direction of your heart,
Then you will always make the right decision,
Even when it doesn't appear you have.

The heart doesn't understand results.
It has a wider frame of reference.
It looks to what is eternal for answers.

36.

Learn to release your concepts.
The sooner you realize that you don't know what you're
doing,
The better off you'll be,
And the more help you will be to your child.
It is not weak to realize you need help.
Weakness is thinking you know something
When you really don't.

Surrendering everything is the beginning of wisdom.
Trusting everything is the foundation of wisdom.
Being grateful for everything is the result of wisdom.

Your children know enough to ask you for help
Even with the smallest decisions.
You would do well to imitate them.

37.

Live securely in the
"I don't know."

38.

You still believe that time is an obstacle to learning.
Time has nothing to do with learning.
Knowing something is the demonstration that you have learned it.
All you are being asked to learn is that you are loved by God.
Your children already know this
But you are still struggling.
You can help your children by allowing them to teach you this.
Then they will embrace it even more completely.

When your child embraces his gifts,
It will ignite something within you that will awaken
Your own knowingness.

Remember that you are in this together.
It is the most important thing we can teach you.

39.

The Psychic Children do not emphasize one gift over
another.
One child may move objects with her mind,
While another heals with his heart.
In either case the gift is motivated by one quality:
Love!

Do not expect your children to perform miracles.
Love is the only miracle that is required.
They are watching you this moment,
And need you to demonstrate this to them.
It isn't because they don't understand it,
But because it creates a bridge between their heart
And their mind.
You are the bridge they need,
And they will return the favor a thousand times.
They cross the bridge from one direction,
And you cross it from the other.
The key is to meet in the middle.

40.

There is no Light at the end of the tunnel.
It is not so far away,
Or anywhere outside your own experience.
It is within you now.
It has never left its source,
Just as you have never left the Mind of God.

There is nowhere for you to go,
Nothing left for you to accomplish.
Reach your hand out to your children
And then stand very still together.
Breathe in very deeply,
And know that you are Home.

Give them permission to be who they are.
This is one of the greatest gifts you can offer your children.
Some of them are coming into the world confused,
Not because they have forgotten,
But because they do not see the love they feel
Reflected in the world.
You are the first place they will look to find this.
If you are open and give them what they need,
Then they will find it everywhere.

41.

Are you willing to forget all the roles you think you have,
Especially when it comes to your children?
Lay them aside and open your heart like a faucet.

There are days when you will be asked to be the parent,
And others when you will be asked to be the child.
Some days you will teach and other days you will learn.
You already know how to set a good example.
Now you must learn how to be weak.
Now you must learn to allow.
Now you must learn how to accept that everything is perfect
Just the way it is.

Don't try to change anything.
Just allow yourself to be changed.

42.

Everything we have to say can be summed up in a few words:

Open.
Allow.
Surrender.
Ask.
Watch.
Listen.
Remember.
Be.
Love.

Anything more would be redundant.

43.

You may think that you need more information
to assist your children in realizing their gifts.
You need less information
And more knowledge.

Information can only get in your way.
There is no answer that will apply to every child,
Or every situation.
You are being asked to let go of what you think,
And realize what you know.
You can do this by watching your child.
It comes naturally when you spend more time being,
And less time becoming.

A Guide for Raising Your Child

by Mary Bell Nyman

When I was three years old, my mother was killed in a car crash. She left five children under the age of six. We were devastated because she was physically gone, but comforted because she hung around us as a spirit for several years until she thought we were strong enough to be on our own. We all saw her spirit clairvoyantly but talking about it ceased because the adults kept telling us she was gone. The thing I remember most about her as a spirit was she radiated a soft, gold energy of love and compassion. I often felt her gentleness enfold me and was deeply comforted by her, even though I cried for her body to return. Because I experienced her so clearly, I never lost my ability to see a spirit in or out of a body. That was a tremendous gift to me from her.

I often fought sleep as a young child because of several spirits that were hanging around in our house. Even now I remember them clearly. I saw these spirits as a deep, navy blue molecular-like energy that moved through the rooms. They were so sad, that I was often frightened of them. They were lower level beings, stuck in the astral plane who wanted to communicate. A spirit, just like a person, can be stuck in such a low vibration that they can't see anything happier or brighter than the dense depression or sadness around them. As adults, we have several choices in how we handle these people, but at the age of three and without the psychic training I have now, I didn't understand how to work with them. I was told every night that no one was there and yet I could see them. The adults got angry with me if I talked about spirits, but I couldn't help it! Little did I know that being able to see spirits and knowing that each of us is a spirit living in a body, would change my life as I grew older. My greatest tragedy became my greatest gift; I have used this ability to work with spirit in education, meditation, and in hospice, where I help people die peacefully.

After graduating from college, I worked with multi-handicapped children, including children who were deaf and blind. As a speech therapist, eliciting communication from and reaching these kids emotionally was my greatest challenge, until I remembered a childhood game my brothers and sister and I had played. We sent telepathic thoughts and mental image pictures to each other and tried to guess what the other sibling was thinking. When I tried the same game with these children they responded with delight! They couldn't hear my words but they could read my thoughts and became aware that I could read theirs. I learned a lot about listening and respecting the feelings and needs of these children. Using my intuition, it became easier to respond to the kids, and they made excellent progress.

I later took classes in meditation and clairvoyant reading at the Berkeley Psychic Institute (BPI). BPI was created by Lewis Bostwick as a sanctuary for psychic, sensitive people in 1975. People learned how to use and refine their psychic skills. I was taught that we each have a personal energy space, called an aura, and each person is responsible for keeping his space "clean" and full of only his or her energy—no one else's. We are "energy sponges" who are unknowingly picking up the feelings, thoughts, and energies of people we interact with, care about, or think about during the course of a day. I learned at BPI that feeling only my own energy—with nobody else's energy inside my space—felt really good! This didn't mean I disconnected emotionally from people I loved; in fact, I was able to feel more love because I had more of my own energy to give. It meant I could return people's energies to them in a gentle, friendly way, and reclaim my own from all the people and places where I'd sent it over the years. This improved my health and my sense of well being. Best of all, these techniques were easy—and fun!

Lewis's wife, Susan, founded the children's psychic school, Yin Yang, after her two children were born. She developed most of the curriculum we used with the kids, creating a school that would validate children's spirits along with their minds. When I took over the school in 1980, we had five children and over the years it developed into three pre-schools. My partner, Natasha Lynn, ran the two elementary schools for psychic children. Over half of these children were born in our birth center run by the Church of Asclepion, affiliated with BPI. I learned how to be a spiritual midwife (one who works with the spirit of the child instead of the body) and was present when a number of these babies came into the world. We started our communication with the spirit of the child while it was in utero. A team of clairvoyants would read the family agreements and look to see why this particular spirit was joining this family and what each person hoped to learn from one another. It was wonderful to have that communication with the baby as a spirit. When the little body finally arrived, the baby would open its eyes and there would be the spirit we had been communicating with for nine months, saying hello telepathically. The baby was so excited to be here and loved that it was honored and recognized as both a spirit and a body. As a clairvoyant spiritual midwife, I noticed that while a spirit is waiting to take a body, it anchors into the left eye of the mother. The spirit moves back and forth between the Godhead and this new body, finishing old karma and clearing the way for this new life. Here we have a spirit with lifetimes of information and a brand new body. The spirit fully integrates into the body between the first and second years. As a child grows, he uses all his pastlife information, and merges his spiritual knowledge with his new physical body. Just like you can remember what you were doing five years ago, so can a one-year-old. Much more of their awareness is in the spiritual realm than in the physical body. In the first four years, children rely more on their spiritual information than on the body's life experience. In most children, it is around age six that the body gets programmed to accept the physical reality over the spiritual one. We all came in as psychic children; our spiritual abilities never go away, they just get covered over with invalidation and non-permission to communicate our truth. Psychic means "soul essence" and being psychic means being your innate spiritual self.

One of the many miracle birth stories involved a baby who was in a difficult breech position. The clairvoyant team communicated with him to rotate in the womb, and one hour later, he was born headfirst. Another story is of Pamela, who was born at home surrounded by her family with several of us holding space for her birth. She was a playful spirit and telepathically gave her mom encouragement throughout the labor process. Funny things happened that made us all laugh. An alarm clock went off that hadn't been set, a delivery man came with a package that had three yellow ducks in it but no gift card of any kind, and the family cat knocked over a box of ping pong balls that scattered all over the floor. We laughed and told stories the whole day so when Pamela arrived, all of us were in high spirits and felt blessed. I swear she was smiling at us a minute after she was born and she continues to have a great sense of humor as a young adult. Each birth was unique and each family felt blessed to have their child born into so such love and acknowledgement. We validated both the spirit as well as the body, and were ahead of our time by creating a sacred sanctuary for our children to experience life from both perspectives. Each child was declared a free spirit before the umbilical cord was cut, and validated as a spirit for what they came to manifest this lifetime. When a child has both sides honored from day one, they grow in love and certainty, and carry that grace with them their whole lives.

The Yin Yang Seminaries for psychic children were located in Santa Rosa, Berkeley, and San Jose, California. Yin Yang was considered part of BPI. As a graduate of BPI, I combined my teaching skills with my psychic abilities. All the teachers at Yin Yang were unique in that they were all trained in clairvoyance and completed a minimum three years of training as a clairvoyant healer and psychic reader. The children ranged in age from six months to 12 years and were able to validate, explore, and own their personal spiritual abilities.

The teachers were the guides, and the children were the creators. As psychic teachers, we communicated with the spirit of the child, recognizing the eternal soul present in a little body. We acknowledged the free will of each spirit and what their spiritual intent was for this lifetime. Children were not taught how to be psychic—they already were! The goal of meditation was to get the child to focus on his own world, to look within for answers to the problems in his universe, and separate other people's energy, ideas, and concepts from his. Doing so freed the spirit of the child so that he could innocently explore the world with new eyes. Creative expression, discovery, and scientific examination become magical when the child is the explorer, open to all experience and given permission to find his own truth.

Teachers were trained to use their psychic tools to create a safe haven for children where they could use their natural psychic abilities. The children were also trained in the academic areas of math, reading, writing, science, language, socialization skills, and problem solving. Allowing children space and permission to grow and have all the knowledge they acquired from past lives, in their present body, was an essential part of the process at Yin Yang. We served as spiritual guides who helped the children discover and enhance their spiritual autonomy and communication with the Source—God. Unfortunately, due to the rising cost of liability insurance, the schools closed in the early1990's.

I would like to share some of the techniques for meditating and some of the psychic games we played so that parents and educators may begin to understand how to communicate with the spirit of a child. Anyone can learn these tools and practice them with their children or students. I will also share some of the daily routines we did at Yin Yang, and the levels of spiritual communication we offered all of the families. Hopefully, in years to come, all children will be educated as both a spiritual being and a body.

Each morning, as a child said good-bye to his parents at the classroom door, he learned to make spiritual separations. This meant pulling his energy out of his parents' space, allowing them to have their day, and also sending the parents' energy back to them, from his space. This is like hanging up the phone and disconnecting until you see each other again. It gives both parents and children freedom to enjoy being themselves until they come back together at the end of the day. Children disconnected by putting their parent's energy in an imaginary soap bubble and releasing their energy with an "I love you, Mom, I love you, Dad, see you later," and popping it. They used an imaginary magnet to call their energy back from their parents' space as well. I observed that because each person had space, neither parent nor child felt guilty about having to leave each other for the day. Before entering the classroom, the child learned to ground and match the energy set for the day. By grounding, I mean making an energy connection from the base of the spine to the center of the earth. Children like to imagine a monkey tail, a giant redwood tree, a flower, waterfall, or merry-go-round pole, to use for a grounding cord. This allows any foreign energy to be released, making it easy for the spirit of the child to be present inside her body. When children matched the energy of the school, it meant matching a vibration set for permission to learn and discover for themselves. This vibration was usually a color: blue for certainty, pink for happiness, green for growth, etcetera. This allowed the child to separate from home and say "hello" to school, being present (right here) in the moment. As she entered the classroom, she experienced moving from her independent workspace to group lessons to stations in the post office, library, store, computer, measuring centers, sewing, art, or listening centers. These workstations are similar to those used in Montessori schools. The child also prepared and served snacks which involved many skills, including solving problems in incredible ways. Here is one of my favorite examples. One child was "snack person." This involved putting a mat and cup with each child's name on it on the table, then filling the cup with juice and passing out graham crackers. Lisa, a three-year-old, was snack person and began filling the cups with juice. Several cups she filled to the brim and then the remaining cups contained only drops of juice. Instead of trying to cut in with adult energy and fix it, I waited to see what would happen. As the kids came to eat, several complained they didn't have juice. The ones with the full cups poured theirs into the empty cups (now considering these was mostly two- and three-year-olds, a lot of the juice graced the tables!) The kids who had very little juice thanked them and all agreed it was a good thing there were sponges! Watching how children heal conflict and solve problems always impressed me. Left to their own, they figure it out and are so gentle with each other.

The children also participated in three meditation circles a day. The first was a morning circle where they said hello to their own space (a bubble or aura) and called their energy into their body. They also owned the space called Yin Yang—again, remembering that the energy of the school was set for the children, not the adults. The next circle (mid-day) was a business circle, where meditation skills were used and business was shared with fellow classmates. The children showed a deep respect for each other's individual space. They learned to use conflict resolution to solve their differences instead of fighting, and they became adept at expressing their feelings and getting their needs met. The last meditation was a closing circle that ended their day at school and prepared them for returning home. Meditation teaches a child to go within and say hello to his own universe. Here, a child defines his physical and spiritual space with a bubble. (Adults call this the aura.) By allowing the child to have and enjoy his bubble, he learns permission to allow others their own space. Children who are in their bodies learn more quickly and have more fun. It gives them the permission to be themselves and to manifest what they came to do this lifetime.

When we taught children to meditate, it worked well because we had been meditating for several years ourselves. All the teachers knew how to go within themselves to a silent space, turn off the noise in their minds, and just be present with themselves. Here in this quiet space, we discover the spirit part of ourselves. It was easy for us Yin Yang teachers to give ourselves a quick healing to release unneeded energy so we could meditate and have our attention on ourselves.

Children meditate the same way. They sit with their eyes closed, in silence, grounded to the earth, becoming more aware of themselves. The morning circle would open with a child ringing a bell while another child lit a candle. A third child held a picture board depicting kids meditating and asked the other children to ground their bodies, make a bubble, and be inside themselves. Next they would create a rose (an energetic protection tool), finish their business, and fill in with a gold sun (an energy tool to replenish the body).

Energy takes no effort to move. It is similar to plugging an electrical cord into a wall socket. Even though we don't see the electricity move through the electric cord, we know it is there because of the outward manifestation of light. When the grounding cord is plugged into the center of the earth, the energy in the body flows like water, allowing anything foreign to be released and your body to be filled with life-force energy. Children made their grounding cord as big around as their hips and had fun trying on many different kinds of grounding cords. They also learned to ground their own classroom, making the grounding cord as wide as the room.

To heal themselves, they began by putting an imaginary washcloth in one ear and out the other, pulling it back and forth to clean out the center of their head. When everyone else's energy is out of their head, children find it easy to visualize and see the answers to problems. Children learn how to validate their own work, take responsibility for what they create, and enjoy that creation. Instead of learning and trying to please someone outside themselves, they took great delight in learning for self-discovery. They weren't guilty if they made a mistake but saw it as a positive part of the discovery process. Instead of becoming critical they remained curious; curiosity opened kids up where critical energy closed them down. We found children stayed excited and open to learning all school year.

The aura is a big bubble around the body. It is sort of like a magnet and sometimes things get attracted to the bubble and stick there. With their eyes closed, children looked inside their bubble to check on its color each day. They cleaned out their bubble with an imaginary sponge, wringing any yucky energy down their grounding cord and into the center of the earth. (Here the energy was transmuted back into neutral energy and given to the earth.) They filled their bubble with a special color that felt right to them along with a quality of energy. This could be blue happy energy or pink flower energy, for example. Children learned to see who was visiting inside their bubble and then sent that person's energy back to them, owning the bubble as their own space.

Next they created imaginary soap bubbles, filled them with energy and popped them, releasing the energy back to a neutral form. They worked a lot on dichotomies; foods they liked or didn't like, things that made them happy or sad, things they liked about being an older sibling and things they didn't like. This gave them permission to own both sides of an issue and work through it.

Then they created a rose just outside their space. The rose symbolizes individual autonomy. It reminded them of good psychic manners, keeping their own energy in, and holding the boundary of their own space. This is similar to the yard around a house with the sidewalk marking the end of the property and the common area of the street. Children enjoyed putting up a rose and letting it mark the edge of their space. When their space was clear and just the way they wanted it, they would fill in with a big gold sun (the size of their whole body) full of happy energy and go about their day. This gold sun energy was their own unique life force and helped the kids maintain optimal health. The Yin Yangers were rarely ever sick.

These children were also consciously clairvoyant. They were aware of their astral travels, could talk about their dreams, past lives, and gave each other healings. But most of all, they had permission from the day they were born, to be themselves. They were recognized as eternal beings, who returned to a human life on Earth and were treated with honor and respect. Children give back what they learn, and the Yin Yangers were full of love and life; even now as they enter their twenties, they walk in grace.

We also worked with each family as a unit, offering spiritual counseling by looking at how the family relates as a whole to the child. In this spiritual counseling, or family reading, the teacher clairvoyantly read the agreements between family members. As a spirit, each of us agreed to come and be part of our family and to learn certain lessons together. When families learn to communicate as spiritual beings in bodies, they begin to give each person space to create their own life experience rather than becoming responsible or controlling of each other. Each person in the family finds their unique expression of their own path, communicating through love, growth, encouragement, and amusement. Because the parents understand what the spirit of their child came to learn this lifetime, they gently guide them on their path. Parents also learn how to be generous towards themselves and nurture themselves while being a parent, creating a win-win situation for the whole family.

This was the basic format we used when working with the children and their families. Many miraculous things happened as the children found permission to be themselves—souls manifesting through their bodies. One of my favorite stories is about a girl I will call Ann. One day I found myself teaching but was tired and not feeling well. I decided to take the kids on a library field trip for some new books. It would be an easy way to end the day and fun for all of us, but I wanted to find the old books to return.

While sitting in front of a bookcase and searching for "Farmer John goes To the Barnyard," I was frustrated because I had twelve of the thirteen books I wanted. Ann walked up to me and suddenly I felt heat pulsing in my hand. I looked down, only to see her materialize the missing book in my hand, molecule by molecule, complete with library card! Nothing in my life had prepared me for that experience! I was just flabbergasted. Blown away. Dumbfounded. Then she looked at me, with a twinkle in her eye, and asked if she could ride in the front seat with me when we went to the library. (I hadn't even said we were going to the library yet.) What could I do? I said yes!

I couldn't talk about what happened that day for awhile. It rocked my whole sense of reality, and I had no explanation for it. I just knew that I had experienced it and I wasn't crazy. Later the next week, Ann went to Mexico with her family for a vacation. While there, she was playing with her mother's earrings and lost one. Her mom scolded and reminded Ann that she had not asked permission to wear them and the earrings were not hers. Later that day, they went down to the restaurant for lunch. Her dad felt a funny vibration under his menu and lifting it, discovered the missing earring. Ann looked at him and said, "Now mommy can't be mad at me." Needless to say, Ann got our attention.

The last time she materialized something, that I know of, was at Sunday school. They were having apples and raisins for snack and she wanted graham crackers. The Sunday school teacher explained to her she didn't have any crackers, but would get them for the next week. Ann then materialized a pack of graham crackers in her hand, and seeing her, another girl did the same thing. It surprised all of us, but we took it in stride. We protected the children so they wouldn't be exploited. None of us had set out to teach those types of psychic abilities to the children; it happened because the energy of school was set at permission to discover and no one ever told these children they had physical limitations. Amazed as we were, we all chose to keep it in house, so to speak. As a young child, Mark used to levitate toys. He didn't do it often, but we captured it on film as he lazily played with one of his toys, turning it around in the air. These kids just demonstrated that all children are more capable than we give them credit for.

Not every child used its psychic abilities in the way Ann and Mark did. Some of the more common things happened at the lunch table. Paul once said to Lizzy, "Remember when you were a boy and I was a girl and we lived in China?" He went on to relate it to whatever they were doing, but my ears perked up when I heard his question. It was fun to hear them speak of their past lives; we never tried to elicit that information but rather gave them permission to speak openly about their experiences. Another strong ability the kids had was healing. Healing means the ability to make a change, spiritually or physically. Once I was meditating and trying to get rid of a migraine headache. A two-year-old came up to me and said, "Your mom's in your head." With that she put her little hand on my head and pulled energy out of my space, instantly ending the migraine I had been trying to heal for over two hours in a split second! I was amazed. Then she asked me if I would play with her. Absolutely!

Ramon taught me a lesson about healing I will never forget.

He was on the playground while the rest of the children were lined up at the gate, ready to go in from recess. Ramon ran up to us, but tripped and slid face first into the gate breaking two boards. That was a hard head! He scraped the whole side of his face into a bloody mess. I jokingly pointed out to Ramon that he had two new healing projects—healing his face and fixing the gate! All the kids stood around Ramon as blood trickled down his face and asked, "What should we do?" Ramon became our science project. After cleaning off his face, we put some of his blood on a slide and looked at it under a microscope. When we were all through, Ramon used his hand to direct his own healing energy to his face. Then, he went outside with a hammer and nails and had a grand time fixing the gate. The next day when Ramon came to school, there was no sign of the scrape from the day before—he had completely healed it. If I hadn't seen it with my own eyes, I wouldn't have believed it. I guess Ramon took his healing project pretty seriously!

Lee Ann woke her parents up to her screaming one morning and was in a state of semi-consciousness. She was talking about a little girl who was dying somewhere in a house fire. She was in anguish because of the little girl's pain. Try as they might, her parents could not get Lee Ann to wake up. About ten minutes later, the girl died and Lee Ann snapped out of the dream-like state. "She's gone now, it's okay," she told her parents. "I had to help her." They could only wonder who the child was and how Lee Ann was connected to her. Once she was awake, she took it all in stride, and went about her day as usual. Her only comment was that the girl had been her best friend once. The parents never did figure out who the mystery girl was. Another little girl named Missie, arrived at school one day and announced her mom was pregnant with a baby boy and his name was Todd. I congratulated the mom at the close of school, only to hear her tell me she wasn't pregnant. The next morning, she came in looking rather embarrassed and told me she had taken a home pregnancy test and guess what? She was pregnant. Eight months later Todd was born. These types of stories happened all the time. When I first started with the Yin Yang children there were only five of them, so in our meditation circle, I suggested we call in their friends, and expected to have some more two-year-olds arrive at the school. Instead, the next month 10 women in our community found out they were pregnant! Never under estimate the power of children!

When Michael was two years old he painted a picture with a toothbrush that looked like nothing more than lines until he made the final downward stroke, adding on a mane and front leg. He looked up at me and said, "horse." It was an incredible picture that looked like a Japanese line painting. I couldn't believe a two-year-old had created the picture in front of me. Children have no limits and they taught me this over and over again. One morning I came to school in a lousy space. I had had a disagreement with my boyfriend, was low on cash, and feeling pressure from all sides. Typical life issues for most of us. When I took the children in to meditate that morning, they politely waited until everyone was seated and then they all got up and walked out of the room. When I asked where they were going, they told me very nicely that my energy was yucky that day and they did not want to meditate with me. Busted by two-year-olds! I could only agree with them and meditated until my space was clear again and we all resumed our day. I loved them for their honesty. They did not judge me, just stated the facts as they saw them. They gave me time to get it back together just like all the days I had done the same for them. It didn't matter that I was the teacher. Another time, I had a toothache. There were no substitute teachers available that day so I had to teach anyway. I gathered all the kids together and told them I wasn't feeling good and asked them to be gentle with me that day. They were amazing. They played and read books and the day flew by. I was off to the dentist office before I knew it. As a team, we helped each other.

Children all around the world are tuned in psychically and aware of each other. Little ones under age three are the most capable psychics on the planet! And guess what? They aren't trying or taking it seriously. They are playing! When I teach a clairvoyant class for adults, the hardest part is getting people out of effort so they can actually see clairvoyantly. Once they begin to play with energy and relax, their clairvoyant abilities open right up. All of us have a mental image picture-making machine in the back of the head, similar to a slide projector. With children, the images are focused one at a time and they are able to read and send mental image pictures quite clearly. In adults, the energy gets jammed up and it is like trying to see a slide in a projector where there are five slides crammed into one slot. Then all you see is black! Once the logjam is cleared, an adult can see just as well. Seeing these pictures and communicating them to someone is what a clairvoyant does when they give a psychic reading. As adults, we sit down and do a formal reading, but children are reading all the time. They constantly make running comments on people they meet, asking the darnedest questions and saying the most outrageous things, most of which are true! All of us have been amazed at some of the things kids come up with. It takes an awesome parent to not turn that ability off in them. Instead, a parent can learn to enhance it and teach them when it is appropriate to communicate certain things.

The best way to teach children to enhance their abilities and keep them is to learn to do it yourself and make it part of your everyday language. For example, each morning when you wake up, ask your child about their dreams and what they mean to them. As a parent, listen. Instead of putting an adult interpretation on it, see what they come up with. Then, as you go about your day, include energy tools as well as physical ones. Talking out loud, you can mention you have a blue tree grounding cord today, so your energy is strong and happy that day. Children may acknowledge what color theirs is as well, or not, either way is okay. But you better believe they will be looking to see if what you're saying is true! Later when you get into the car, you can ask what kind of grounding cord should be given to the car for a safe journey to the store. Let them choose one and help you. After shopping, you can say, "I'm calling all my energy back to my bubble and saying good-bye to the store." They will imitate you whether they voice it or not. It isn't like you have to do a running commentary on your energy tools all day. Just mention them several times a day, just like you would say, "Okay it's time to put on our shoes to go to the store." You blend the two worlds together so they have permission to have both of them. As adults, we can help hold open the door to spirituality so that our children don't have to lose touch with their spiritual side as they grow up. The Maori Indians in New Zealand insisted the school board allow spiritual information be taught in the classroom as well as the academic material, because their children weren't capable of separating the two sides. Perhaps in the future, many more of us will create schools that teach the whole child—spirit, mind, and body. Having accomplished it in the 1980's, I know we can do it again.

Mary Bell Nyman teaches meditation, healing, and clairvoyant classes, and does clairvoyant readings through the Psychic Horizons Center in Boulder, Colorado. She formerly directed three pre-schools and two elementary schools for the Berkeley Psychic Institute in the San Francisco Bay Area. She has worked extensively with clairvoyantly gifted children, and multi-handicapped children. For more information about her work: contact Mary Bell Nyman, 1535 Spruce St. Suite 123, Boulder, CO 80303, USA, 303-440-7171.)

44.

Laugh often.
Tell silly jokes.
Smile at strangers.
Ask lots of questions.
Be willing to look stupid.
Take time to observe nature.
Let a dog lick you in the face.
Ask for help when you need it.
Lay in the grass and watch clouds.
Go for a walk even when it is raining.

These are the things that your children need to see you do.
It helps them accept who they are,
And helps you remember who you once were.

45.

Open your heart and Pretend that everything we are saying
is true.
There is still a part of you that wonders,
Otherwise you wouldn't need to hear it at all.
This book would be unnecessary.
Pretend that you and your child are waking up together.
Then you'll realize that there is no gift you will give,
That you don't receive.
Then you'll understand the simple truth
That you are not alone or separate.
Your child has come to bring you a gift,
But you cannot receive that gift until you give it to her.
Are you beginning to understand?

Pretend that you are one with your child.
Then you will be very close to a much deeper truth,
That you are one with everyone else,
And with God.

This is not a concept you can understand with your mind.
It simply is what it is.

46.

Your willingness to Pretend
Is an opening into the mind of your child
And will help you understand what he needs.
That is why you are here now,
And it is why you are reading this book.
As a parent you want to give your child every chance
To fulfill his purpose on this planet.
He wants the same thing for you,
Though he may not realize this with his mind.
It is what his soul is calling for.

To Pretend is to become like a child again.
How can you help your children
If you aren't willing to see through their eyes?

Try to think with a mind that is new to this world.
Try to remember how it felt when the veil was thin,
And you were able to perceive something that
Your eyes could not see.
It is your holiness you have forgotten,
And you will remember your own by seeing your child's.

When you realize God loves you,
Then your gift will be pure.

47.

Just because you are Pretending something
Doesn't mean it isn't true.
There is no difference between your visions of reality
And reality Itself.
Children understand this.

48.

Your children know that life is a game.
There is no such thing as winning or losing,
Only playing well.
How will you know how well you have played this game?
Are you happy?
That is the only question you need to ask yourself.
How can you expect your child to hold onto this vision
If you don't remember it yourself?

Be happy even when you're not.
If you can understand what this means,
Then you're further along than you think.

49.

You are not living in a literal universe.
I mean that quite literally.
You have made up everything you see.
Are you willing to go that far?
If you are,
Then you are very close to where you need to be,
Not to help your child,
But to wake up.
That is the only thing that will help your child.

How can you take care of your child's physical needs
If you are asleep in your bed?
Likewise,
How can you attend to her deeper needs
If you are spiritually asleep?

You cannot expect her to realize her gifts
Until you open your eyes and leave your dreams behind.
This is why I keep saying that this is more about you
Than your child.

50.

Perhaps you are beginning to finally understand that the
Only way you can help your child realize his Gifts
Is to realize your own.

You may not want to hear that message,
But it is the only truth you need to embrace for now.
It is easier to be given a list of exercises or meditations.
You may be satisfied with this,
But your child won't.
He needs you!
Don't think that sacrificing your own joy
Increases his.
The more you allow yourself to receive,
The more you will be able to give.

That's the kind of example he needs.

51.

Do not hold these ideas too tight in your hand.
It's the surest way to lose them.
Open up your heart and let them flow in and out.
This is how the universe responds to truth,
And it is how your children play.

Reality to them is not rigid or straight.
It is soft and round.
There are no real definitions,
But open spaces into which everything flows.

Learn to look at the world in this way,
And then you will know the best way you can help them
grow.

52.

The only way you can really help your children
Is by realizing that they are fine just the way they are.
Then perhaps you'd be willing to give that same gift to
yourself.

Then you would realize that you're fine just the way you are.

You don't need to change a thing.
It will lead to your freedom.
You don't need to go anywhere,
Or do anything at all.
It will lead to your enlightenment.

When you allow your mind to be filled with Light,
You are giving your child permission to do the same.

This article is excerpted from from
The Ancient Secret of the Flower of Life, Volume II.

The Emergence of Super Psychic Children

by Drunvalo Melchizedek

The super psychic children are perhaps the most unusual and charismatic race being born today. Their dramatic abilities distinguish them from the other two races with their sensational demonstrations. These children are able to do things that most people thought could be done only in movies with computer graphics. What is the most amazing of all is that it is real. If these children don't change our world, nothing will. Notice how some of the abilities of these children resemble the manifestations of consciousness we talked about in chapter 18, during the dimensional shift. What you think is what you get! These children are able to demonstrate that whatever they think becomes reality.

Paul Dong and Thomas E. Raffill wrote a book called, China's Super Psychics. It reports what has been transpiring in China around these new psychic children who began to emerge in 1974 with the young boy who could see with his ears. Actually, the Chinese government claims that these children, when blindfolded, could see either with their ears, nose, mouth, tongue, armpits, hands, or feet. Each child was different and their vision from these unheard-of areas was perfect. These tests were not just a percentage right some of the time; they were flawless.

I first spoke about these children in 1985 when I mentioned the article about them in Omni magazine. Omni was invited to come to China to observe some of these children and write an article about them. Omni assumed that there might be cheating involved, so when they were given some of these children to test, they conducted their examinations in a way that ruled out any possible cheating. They left nothing to chance.

One of the tests began this way: With the children present, Omni took a stack of books and at random selected one of them, then opened the book at random and ripped out a page, crumpling it up into a small ball. Omni then placed it in the armpit of one of these children—and this child could read every word on the page perfectly! After many varied tests, Omni became convinced that the phenomenon was real, but they could not explain how these kids were doing it. Their report was released in their January 1985 issue.

Omni was not the only one to send researchers to observe these children. Several other world magazines and respected journals such as Nature, a prestigious science magazine, have agreed that this phenomenon is real.

In Mexico City we found exactly the same new human traits emerging in the children there. There may be more, but we found over one thousand children able to see with various parts of their bodies. What is noticeable is that these Mexican children can see with the very same parts of the body as the Chinese children. It sounds like this DNA mutation has jumped across the ocean just as in the hundredth-monkey phenomenon. I will come back to one of these children, now nineteen, to give my direct experience of the abilities she demonstrated to us.

According to Paul Dong in China's Super Psychics, seeing with various parts of the body was the psychic ability that caught the attention of the Chinese government, but this ability was quickly understood to be only the tip of the iceberg. These children began to demonstrate other psychic abilities that are truly difficult to accept inside this "normal" reality.

Mr. Dong reports how several times a large audience of a thousand people or more would enter the auditorium and be handed a live rosebud. When everyone was seated and quiet, the demonstration would begin with a young Chinese girl, about six years old, who would come on stage all by herself and stand in the center facing the audience. Then with a silent wave of her hand, the thousand rosebuds would slowly open into full-blown, beautiful roses before the eyes of the astonished audience.

Mr. Dong also speaks of how over five thousand young children have demonstrated another amazing feat in public. Realize that the Chinese government has carefully tested these children to see if what I am about to say is real or not. The government is convinced it is.

One child would take a sealed bottle of pills off a shelf at random, like vitamin pills, for example. The bottle would be sealed with the original plastic wrap and have a tightly screwed metal or plastic top. The bottle would then be placed in the center of a large, bare table. Then a video camera would observe what happened next.

The child would say to the audience that he/she was beginning, but nothing was visible to the audience. Suddenly, the pills inside the sealed bottle would pass right through the glass and appear on the table. In many cases, the child would then take another object, such as a coin, set it on the table, and it would pass into the sealed bottle. This demonstration and others like it are definitely approaching what I would call fourth-dimensional consciousness. What you think and what happens are connected.

There are several other psychic abilities that have been demonstrated in China, according to the book. If you are interested, read what has been reported. You may think that these are just magic tricks, but when you see these things in person, they are very hard to explain. For the first ten years, the Chinese government would not believe them either, until the number of children who could do these things kept growing. By the time China's Super Psychics was released in 1997, the Chinese government had identified over one hundred thousand of these children. In fact, by about 1985, the government and the Chinese scientific community simply had to admit they were real.

Because they realized what this could mean, the government

set up training schools to assist these children in their psychic abilities. Whenever a psychic child is found now, he or she is sent to one of these schools. Important is the fact that they have found that they can even take children who are not known to be psychic and in the presence of the naturally psychic kids, the trained children can perform the same amazing feats.

This brings forth the memory of Uri Geller, the famous psychic from Israel who could bend metal objects just by looking at them. In his book, Uri Geller, My Story, he talks about when he demonstrated his psychic abilities on television throughout Europe. He went on TV and asked people to get knives, spoons, and forks and place them in front of the television set. With millions of witnesses, he bent tableware in the studio as well as tableware in the homes of people who were watching the show. This single act had an interesting side effect. From the phone calls immediately after the show and the following days, it was discovered that over fifteen hundred children were able to do the same thing just by seeing it happen one time. They could all bend the metal tableware with their minds.

People, especially scientists, were convinced that Mr. Geller was a magician and that everything he did was a trick of some kind. Stanford Research Institute asked if he would submit his magic to scientific scrutiny. Mr. Geller agreed. For a period of time Mr. Geller did whatever Stanford asked him to do to prove once and for all that his psychic ability was not a trick.

Just to give you an idea of how tight the testing at Stanford was, one of the tests placed Mr. Geller in a sealed steel room, which was also a Faraday cage (a room where electromagnetic fields, such as radio waves and even brain waves or thoughts, could not pass through the walls). He was sealed in physically as well as energywise. Outside the test chamber, the Stanford researchers placed a sealed, hand-blown glass tube that was twisted on each end so that it could not be opened without breaking it. Inside it was a piece of the hardest metal known to man. Then they told Mr. Geller to bend it. With all their scientific instruments recording the test, Stanford scientists watched in total amazement as the piece of superhard metal bent as if it were Jell-O. Mr. Geller could in no way have cheated.

What is so impressive is that besides Mr. Geller, there were about fifteen children from Europe who could also do these things, and they were tested along with him. Everything that Stanford did to test Mr. Geller they also did with the children, and these kids could do everything he could do. So if this was a trick, then fifteen children were also "advanced magicians," and Stanford Research Institute, with all their scientific magic, could not detect fraud.

This test and the rest of the research from Stanford were printed in Nature magazine in its October 1974 issue. The New York Times immediately came out with an editorial that said: '"The scientific community has been put on notice 'that there is something worthy of their attention and scrutiny' in the possibilities of extrasensory perception." Yet here we are in the next millennium, and science still will not seriously admit that the human potential for psychic abilities is real. I believe that these new children appearing around the world will soon force science into accepting what has always been true. The old paradigm has nowhere to go and must dissolve.

In Denver, Colorado, in July 1999, I spoke about these new children to a large audience. I asked a young woman named Inge Bardor from Mexico to demonstrate directly to this audience her ability to see with her hands and feet. At that time she was eighteen years old. For about an hour, Inge placed a blindfold around her eyes and accepted photographs from the audience. She would hold the photograph and lightly touch it with the fingertips of her other hand.

First she would describe the picture perfectly, as though she was looking at it, but then she would become more specific, giving information that would be impossible for her to know even from a photo. She could tell everything about the people or place in the photo. She could tell exactly where the photo was taken and what was around the area outside the view, such as a lake or buildings. Inge could even describe the person who took the photograph and what he/she was wearing that day. She could tell you what everyone in the photo was thinking at the moment the picture was taken. In one photo of the inside of a house, Inge went into the house psychically and described exactly what was down the hallway. She even described what was on the bedside table.

Finally someone placed a newspaper under Inge's feet, and with her high-heeled shoes on, she was able to read the paper as if it was in her hands. (If you are interested in this video, please call Lightworks Video at 1-800-795-TAPE and ask for Through the Eyes of a Child.)

Under the strict discipline of scientific research, the Chinese government has observed these children changing the human DNA molecule in a Petri dish, before cameras and scientific equipment necessary to record this supposedly impossible feat. If this is true, which the Chinese government claims, would we not be able to change our own DNA with just the right understanding? I think so. Just follow the children.

How is it possible that 60 million people in the world have already changed their DNA to drastically improve their immune systems against HIV infection through spontaneous genetic mutation, if not through a process similar to what our new children of China have demonstrated? This is a grand time in the history of the Earth—and you are alive to experience this extraordinary world change!

Drunvalo Melchizedek is the founder of the Flower of Life Workshops, as well as an author and teacher. To learn more about Drunvalo, visit his web site at >www.drunvalo.net<.

53.

Why do you think we keep saying the same things over and
over?
The Light reflects off a diamond differently
Depending upon how you look at it.
And yet it is the same diamond.
The same is true about reality.
You are about to learn that the whole universe is
Contained within your heart.
Look at it from many different angles
And you will see the whole world.
Then you will understand the Mystery of Life.

Your child's heart is within you as well.
That's why we keep saying that you are the one
Who must accept these truths,
Not your child.
She already knows them.
She is only waiting for you to give her permission
To be herself.

54.

If you realized how simple this is
You would close this book
And throw your arms around your child.
We're not asking you to do anything you aren't doing
already.
We're just asking you to understand why you're doing it.

There is only one reason for helping your child awaken
His psychic gifts.
It helps you remember who you are.
Anything less than this doesn't matter at all.

It is a great mystery you will never understand with your
mind.
But your heart already knows it's true.
Listen to what it has to say.

55.

Your awakening is intimately linked to your child's.

In the end it is the same thing.

This is true for the whole world as well.

In the end there is only one person who needs to wake up.

Guess who it is?

56.

When you open your eyes you are able to see
What has always been in front of you.
When you open your heart
You are able to perceive what has always been true.

We are trying to train you how to think with a heart
That comprehends the eternal nature of things.
How else will you be able to see the soul of your child?
The soul cannot be seen with your eyes,
But with a heart that has been pried open by love.

The more you express your love the longer it will breathe
The intoxicating air of pure freedom.
The longer it breathes this freedom
The less likely it will ever want to return to prison again.

57.

It would be easy to give you instructions
On what to do or how to act toward your child.
It is better to let your soul get thirsty
Until it digs a deep hole into the earth.
Then the water will spring up
And you will never be thirsty again.

You may have thought that this book would be
An instruction manual or a guide on raising psychic children.
It is actually a guide on waking up within the Eternal Truth
Residing in your soul every moment of your life.
Then you won't need these words.

Your children are watching you.
Set a good example by taking this to heart.

58.

These are not ideas that can be understood with your mind,
But jewels that are mined by the soul.
If you want to really help your child,
Stop thinking about it.
Just trust that you already have everything you need.
You have more help than you can even imagine.

There are children all over the world who know about you,
Simply because they know about themselves.
Does this make any sense at all?
It isn't meant to.
It should confuse you enough
That you give up trying to understand
And fall backward into the arms of Grace.
Everything else is guaranteed.

59.

Here's what you can tell your child:
There is nothing in this world worth achieving
But a heart that is always present to the moment.
When that happens,
Everything else falls into place by itself.

What if your child is too young to understand this?
Then show her by the way you live your own life.

60.

The best way to open your heart is to help people.
It doesn't even matter how you do it.
The real gift doesn't belong to the other person.
It belongs to you.

The best way to help your children
Is to provide them with the opportunities they need
To help others.
Do this as quietly as you can.
Don't draw too much attention to yourself,
But allow them to make their own path.
Set a good example,
Then let the Universe do the rest.

TEACHING AND LEARNING WITH TODAY'S CHILDREN

by Sharon Elaine, A.Q.

It must be frustrating for parents who don't understand today's children, to be around them, much less to raise them. They look into their children's clear, determined, yet loving eyes and think "How dare they look me directly in the eyes, as if they are my equal?" It may be the cause of many domestic disputes between parents, children, and teens.

I catch myself berating my 17-year-old daughter for something minor and I see in her eyes such deep clarity and also confusion at my actions. She looks at me as if to ponder "Why is this bothering you?" Granted, teens rarely understand why parents are concerned about things, and yet these new psychic children understand so much more than we did at their age. They are much more mature in so many ways. Unfortunately society agrees with us on this point in the area of their sexuality (younger and younger girls looking older for sexual purposes). Society is very much missing the boat on this one.

The maturity that these young people are emitting is so much more than physical. They reach levels of understanding about the world that literally exude from their being. It's an energy vibration. It is not even something that most of us have a name for yet. It is what I call a Loving Confidence.

Many parents misunderstand this as defiance, so they do their best to beat it out of them (sometimes physically, mostly verbally). They see it as a loss of control to allow their children to have their own minds, and consider it completely disrespectful to suggest that the child might actually have something to teach them.

One thing I've learned from my 17-year-old daughter that fascinates me is her ability to not let things bother her. From having her car not work, to losing out on a job, to watching me yell at her, and more ... she has the ability to see this from a distance and simply observe. She doesn't call it this, and yet it's obvious that is what is occurring. She has an almost confused look on her face when in the midst of these types of daily life experiences. Because of this positive trait, she is able to see all sides of the issue, calmly, and choose the one that feels best to her. She doesn't waste time in regret or worry or irritation. She simply flows with all of life. She refuses to believe in limitations, therefore has embraced so many different skills, she is truly a Renaissance young woman.

My 9-year-old, though very psychic and connected to Source, is not always the perfect child, behaviorally speaking. He DOES get upset at that which he feels he cannot immediately have. It's interesting to me, as it is also an enlightened way to look at life. When something is withheld from him, even for "good" reasons, his eyes flash a momentary "WHY would I be denied anything?" type of look. His innate nature does not believe in limitations, so when he is faced with some, he uses human emotions to demonstrate his non-agreement with such thinking and behavior. He is easily able to get himself out of any kind of negative feeing, however. His young mind simply finds a different way to obtain the goal he seeks. I'm fascinated by the wonderful alternative solutions he has come up with, where he and I both win.

When he was between 2 and 3 years old, I asked him if he had angels. He nodded a big yes, eyes bright and joyful, yet with seriousness beyond his human years. I asked how many, and he answered "three" matter-of-factly, and continued coloring. I asked him if they were with us in the room now, and he said "Yes, Mommy" (like I should have known the answer to this).

I asked him to point them out to me. He sighed (being disturbed from his coloring), looked around, focused in one corner of the ceiling, and pointed, then looked quickly around, pointed again, then pointed right next to him, picked up his crayon and began to color again. I got goose bumps and asked, "Do they have names?" He said "Oh yes, Silky, Snowball, and James." I asked if they were always with him and he said "Silky and Snowball are, James comes and goes when I need him."

Ever since then, his powers of intuition have increased and are quite astounding at times. He knows what I (or others) will say before we say it, and will actually vocalize our thoughts before we do. He knows when people will be coming home and when events will work or not work out.

I feel that ALL children are born with these gifts, but in my childhood, we were taught early on to forget them and reprogram ourselves to this limited environment. The children of today ... Children of Oz, are a stronger evolution, energy-wise, and are going to be able to retain their sense of true self.

My 17-year-old son (yes, I have twins) amazes me in the way he knows everything will work out well for him. He auditions for plays that he knows he will get parts for, music groups he knows will invite him to join, friends and girlfriends he knows will welcome him, and much more. It is not a conscious choosing most of the time; it is also an innate trait of KNOWING. He simply knows it will all work out for him. On the few occasions when this hasn't been the case, he has also taken on the role of observer ... curious as to the oddity of not having his desires manifest. He quickly switches his focus off of that experience and back onto the knowing he will get more of what he desires in the future.

All of my children are such great teachers for me, and I hope I am still somewhat of a teacher for them as well. I have always had a bit of an issue with saying "I'm proud of you" to my children. The reason for this is, it makes it sound like I had something to do with their success. Though I do feel we all help one another on levels we may not be able to see, I feel the children do the majority of the work themselves. I have explained this to my children, and instead use the phrase: "I'm so happy for you" when they tell me of something they have successfully manifested. The greatest gifts I can give them are: freedom, love, open-mindedness, courage, faith and confidence in themselves, and someone who tells them constantly that there are no limitations, except the ones they create in their own minds.

Many parents disagree with my open way of parenting, yet "the proof of the pudding is in the tasting," and my children are prime examples of how this new, open style of parenting works so much better than the shame/guilt/fear-based way of parenting of the past. Some people even feel that if we are not overly strict, that the children will lose respect for us and go wild and crazy. I have found the opposite to be true. They respect my role as their parent in this lifetime, as I respect their role as my child. However, we DO speak to one another on a level of spirit that goes beyond levels and labels ... to the level of equality we share. I look forward to each new year and each new day, and the miracles and joys we all share together

Sharon Elaine, A.Q., is the author of The Book of Affirmations *and has been on the path of self-improvement, metaphysics, spirituality, and journalism for over 25 years. She is a Reiki Master and teacher, a popular public speaker, a spirit channeler, and sends out affirmation/motivation emails twice a week to a group of hundreds on the Internet. She has a growing audio library that turns out a new selection every year. To contact the author, you may email her at >queensef@aol.com<, or check how to order her products on her website >www.invitethelight.net<.*

61.

This is the first thing you will say when you open your eyes
And perceive reality for the first time:
"What took me so long?"

What is true never moves.
You are the one who is dancing,
And the whole world seems to vibrate out of control.
Hold still and you will understand what needs to happen.

Watch your children when they are sleeping.
This will teach you everything you need to know about
stillness.

62.

The questions you ask your children are like keys
That unlock doors in their hearts and minds.
Give them as many keys as you can,
And look inside the rooms they reveal.
You would do well to spend time in all these rooms.
It will help you learn everything you need as well.

63.

If you focus your attention on asking your children
What they need,
Rather than telling them what you need,
Then you will both receive everything you desire.

This sounds very simple.
Putting it into practice may be a bit harder.
It will fulfill you in unseen ways.

64.

You may encounter special challenges in raising sensitive children.
These challenges are unmined jewels,
Or unrecognized gifts.
You are capable of cracking the shell that
Reveals this shining diamond.
But crack your own shell first.

65.

Your children are trying to make their way
Through a forest they do not understand.
That is because they see with eyes that perceive the
World in a new way.
Don't try to correct their vision,
But adopt the same vision for yourself.

66.

Listen to the sounds that come from their mouths
Rather than the words.
Do you understand what I mean by this?
A sigh will tell you more than a thousand words can,
And a single laugh more than a book.

A sound is a direct path to the soul of your child.
It is the heart saying,
"I can't explain this with words,
But it is real to me."
Allow it to be real for you
And you will be giving your child a great gift.

67.

There will be times when your children run from what they know,
And from who they are.
That is because the world has yet to catch up to them,
And they sometimes feel alone.
The best thing for you is to listen to their feelings,
And reflect the truth by the way you live your own life.
Let them know that their feelings are important.

68.

There is no need for you to talk about these things to others.
Hold them in the most sacred place you know.
You don't even need to talk to your children about these things.
The words don't matter anyway.
Open up your heart and live life.
That has been God's message since the beginning of time.
The children are here now to make God's will manifest.

69.

There is a sorrow deep in your children's heart
That even they don't understand.
It is there because their hearts comprehend something
That they do not see reflected in the world.
You and your children share the same goal:
To activate in the world what has always been true in the heart.

You will ease their pain by making it real in your life first.
That's why they chose you to be their parent.

70.

The new children understand conflict more than they do
peace.
Does this surprise you?
They know what has never worked in the world,
Or what has never fulfilled the purpose it was designed to
fulfill.
Peace is full within them,
While within the world of form
It is nothing more than a possibility.
When you abandon your attraction to war,
Then the children will do the same.

71.

Why do you expect your children to exist in a place
You do not choose for yourself?
They are an extension of your mind
Like everything else you perceive.
That is why this book is more focused on you
Than on your children.
They are watching you this very moment.
Give them something that will inspire their way.

Nourishing the Soul of the Psychic Child

By Michael J Tamura

"Truly, I say to you, unless you turn and become like children, you will never enter the kingdom of heaven."
—Jesus the Christ (Matthew 18:3)

Heaven. You can see it in the eyes of little children. Its light burns through the mist of forever and emerges triumphant from those innocent orbs at various moments as laughter, sweetness, honesty or sparkling mischief. Whenever we lose our way to our inner nature and our true priorities in life, children often serve to illuminate our path back. Every child in some unique way reminds us of the heaven we once knew.

When we were children, life spilled out of us in giddy effervescent bucketfuls. Our eyes were bright and shining because they were truly the windows to our soul and someone was really home in that body, fulfilling his or her true purpose. But sooner or later, the assaults of violent tempers, unkind thoughts and ignorant expectations from others took their toll on the sensitive and giving nature of our inner spirit. In order to protect ourselves, we started trying to be something other than who we were. We learned to hide our sacred light ... even from our own selves.

It is written in the Hindu *Upanishad,* "It is not for the love of children that children are dear; but for the love of the Soul in children that children are dear." It is this *soul* that shines so brightly in little children before they learn to hide it from the torment of invalidation. We are, each of us, immortal souls who chose to incarnate in order to explore and discover our true spiritual potential, to realize all that we are and to share our reality with life. The more we can touch our inner spiritual nature, the greater meaning we find in our existence and the more we feel our true worth. Young children naturally tend to be more in touch with their inner being. When we are near them, we feel their deep psychic connection and it lifts our spirit. This is what we so love about them.

Being a Psychic Child

We are all born psychic—aware of and connected to our inner spiritual reality. The word *psychic* means "of the soul." Yet, most of us do not survive psychically intact beyond our first four to seven years of life. As the oft-told story goes with the little girl asking her newborn brother: "Quick! Tell me what God looks like; I'm starting to forget."

Take, for example, my young friend "Alice," a precocious psychic child who used to talk openly with her spirit guides and friends. She would regularly offer profound spiritual insights eons beyond her age. Yet, shortly before her eighth birthday she confided in her mother that she was too embarrassed to talk about "those" things anymore.

Then there is "Jeremy," a nephew of mine. By the time he was seven, he had provided detailed accounts of his previous incarnations as well as how he, as a soul, went about arranging to be born to his parents. One day, however, when he was thirteen, he said to me in despair, "I don't think all those spiritual things I used to say about my past lives are true. No one believes me; they all say I'm just making it up."

I, too, was a psychic child. I knew myself as a spiritual being. I remember "floating" above my mother as the nurses wheeled her into the hospital delivery room. Later, my mother told me that, as a newborn baby, I looked like an old man who had lived years before I was born.

As a child, I already knew I had much to teach others and that I wanted to offer healing. Shortly before her death, my mother revealed that a young man had felt compelled to give her a card reading when she was pregnant with me and had told her that her baby was a healthy boy, a teacher, and a healer. As soon as I could walk, I found myself gravitating toward both children and adults who were suffering or undergoing intensive life transitions.

As a five- or six-year-old, I would "know" what a person was going through—and what was causing his problems. I would know those things every time because certain geometrical patterns appeared in front of me ... and I assumed that everyone else, certainly the person involved, saw the same thing that I did. "Look," I would say pointing to the patterns, "now do you understand what's happening with you?"

Blank stares were all that I ever got back. No one seemed to know what I was talking about. After repeated failed attempts in communicating what I saw, I decided that this way didn't work. And I stopped seeing the patterns.

About the time the geometrical patterns disappeared from my life, I started seeing what I used to call "colored clouds" around people. Of course, I had no one to teach me about "auras" at the time, but I "knew" things about people when I looked at their changing colors. Once again, no one understood what I was saying. And, once again, I decided this manner of communicating with people didn't work. Gradually, the "auras" faded out of my vision as well.

By the time I was in fifth grade, I finally "discovered" how to communicate with people: I had to *intellectualize* everything. Instead of experiencing people through psychic avenues as I had been, I understood that I was expected to make up reasons for the way things were. Many people seemed to prefer to explain things away rather than feel, hear, see, and know. Although all I wanted was to help them heal, many were afraid and wanted instead to hide from their pain. And having a "reason" for everything did just that.

So, I learned to intellectualize. And I began to fulfill others' expectations. Then, instead of being a sensitive and loving yet fumbling, bumbling dummy, I transformed myself into a cool and calculating student. I was "on top" of everything intellectually and garnered awards, respect, and popularity amongst classmates and teachers alike. I had begun to sell my soul piecemeal in exchange for a sense of belonging in this world.

Fortunately, the resulting ache of inner emptiness that I felt quickly prevailed over the transient "highs" of overachievement. By my late teens, I had turned my attention inward, searching for that unnamed something I had left behind in my childhood. I longed to experience a more profound and meaningful life. And I sought out someone who would show me the way.

Lewis, the teacher I finally found, was one of those rare individuals who had never lost sight of that inner connection with which we are all born. He had retained his psychic awareness and abilities during those vulnerable, highly impressionable years of childhood and had emerged as the spiritual teacher he was born to be. He credited several people in his early life as having helped him not forget or lose the psychic connection he had with his inner being. "Each of them," he said, "validated my way of experiencing life at the time I needed it most."

When he was in first grade, for example, Lewis discovered he had a powerful ally in his teacher. One day she assigned everyone in the class to paint a picture of a cat. For the assignment, he had painted a picture of his pet cat as *he* saw it—a purple sphere with green around it ... and his classmates ridiculed him with, *"That's not a cat!"* They snickered and sneered.

His teacher, however, quieted the class and examined the picture. "Lewis has a gift," she told the class. "He has the ability to see beyond the surface of things. He can see what most of us do not." In her own way, she understood that Lewis possessed a high degree of clairvoyance, the ability to see the soul and aura of people and other living things. To him, his cat was not its physical body but the true spirit residing within it, and that was what he had painted. It was a "spirit" portrait instead of a physical one.

I was fortunate to have met Lewis when I was only twenty-one. Under his tutelage, I began to reverse the process of my "forgetting." I began to reclaim my ability to see auras and learned to develop my understanding of what I saw. Unlike the frustration I met as a child in attempting to communicate my awareness without adequate vocabulary or the know-how to put things in perspective, this time, I was able to put the appropriate words and concepts to what I was experiencing psychically. I learned to establish a solid communication with others, even if they were unable to see auras as I did.

Then, after a few years of seeing auras again, the geometrical patterns of relationships began to reappear for me, as well. Even today, few people may relate if I were to describe the geometry of my vision or even the auras that I see, yet now I have the skills to convey what it all means to me in a language that others can understand.

For almost three decades now since Lewis first validated my natural awareness, I have been applying my psychic abilities to help thousands of women, men, and children along their paths of spiritual healing, growth, and fulfillment.

Validating the Psychic Child

We all begin our lives as psychic children, intimately aware of our spiritual existence. Yet, even the most psychic of us tends to "lose" our connection to our inner being, at least for a while. Once we start to forget, some of us may not make any conscious attempts to regain it until we are gasping for the last few breaths of our lives. For others of us, however, the desire to return to our true self is so strong that we are willing to risk humiliation, criticism, and rejection. If we are so willing, then, in one way or another, we will begin to rebuild our psychic bridge of awareness back to our true spiritual birthplace. And, as we do this for ourselves, we can begin to provide the all-important validation and spiritual support for our psychic children as their parents, teachers, healers, and friends.

The validation of his or her spiritual experience and worth that we offer a psychic child may be the single most important ingredient in nurturing and nourishing "the soul in that child." My teacher had received such validation at crucial times during his psychic childhood when his credibility and worth were being challenged. The strength of this support helped him retain his psychic connection with his inner self. As for me, I didn't wait for my connection to dim; I turned off the switch to it when I concluded that it didn't serve its purpose. But, I did return to reclaim it as soon as I received validation that it did work and that I could use my spiritual awareness in everyday life.

How many of us grew up around parents, relatives, teachers, ministers, doctors, and other authorities as well as peer groups of classmates and friends who would deny us of our true psychic experiences of life? How easy was it to have the treasures of our imagination and psychic awareness invalidated by an authoritative voice claiming, "It's just your imagination; it's not real"? A variation of this may have been, "How can you possibly know that; you're just a child?" Or perhaps, "Who told you that?" which implies that you couldn't have known it on your own.

When such doubts are repeated to us often enough by those "who know better," we learn to doubt ourselves as well. The fears that breed such doubts can be contagious.

When my nephew had the doubts clouding the truth of his inner experience and his psychic connection grew dim through constant invalidation, I had the fortune of being able to offer him some validation. I knew that in his state of despair, I couldn't merely *tell* him that what he knew was true and that he wasn't just making it all up. I had to let him experience a little of his own psychic awareness and energy. In order to do so, I asked him if he would give me a psychic reading using the "magic" cards he was fond of collecting. It was not something I had ever even talked about with him before. I just asked him if he would give me a reading on what I needed to be aware of in my life at the time.

Without hesitation, he began shuffling his deck of cards. He laid out four cards that he said represented things that stood out in my life. First, he told me about a problem in my lower back that needed to be taken care of. He didn't know that I had already scheduled a chiropractic treatment since I was aware of the problem. He even accurately pinpointed the exact vertebrae that were involved (which were confirmed later by the chiropractor). Next, he described several people who were in competition with me and were trying to throw roadblocks in my path. I knew exactly whom he was talking about. Then he read that I was soon going to expand my scope of teaching to reach more people. Within a few months of the reading, his prediction came to pass. Finally, he told me that I was going to write a book and that it was going to help a lot of people. At the time, I had only been thinking of writing a book but I hadn't told him anything about my plans.

Once he had finished giving me the reading, he looked up at me and said, "You know, Uncle, I'm pretty sure now that I knew what I was saying when I talked about my past lives and other spiritual things before. It's just that a lot of people have a hard time understanding those things." As he exercised his natural ability to "read" me, he had regained some of his psychic connection and his certainty of what was true for him.

For most psychic children, a little validation of their spiritual experiences and abilities go a long way. Even if you are uncertain of your own psychic nature and experiences, give the child a safe space in which to communicate his inner experiences. Be willing to explore with him his experiences openly and without fear or prejudice. A sanctuary for such communication consists of a genuine sense of permission to express one's experiences without threat of judgment, criticism, or ridicule. It needs to be a haven where the reality of one's experience is not denied. There must be respect along with a playful compassion for the information that is shared in confidence. It will certainly help, too, if you can provide some reassurance that you or others that you know have shared similar experiences. And if you can have the certainty that such experiences are normal, that will further ground that safe environment.

Imaginary Playmates, Ghosts, and Monsters Under the Bed

I haven't known a little child who didn't talk and play with their "imaginary" friends. That is, until it becomes not acceptable for them to do so. Generally parents, teachers, and other adults put a stop to children having such relationships when they reach five to seven years of age. Adults who have had their own psychic connection invalidated during their childhood would believe that their children's "imaginary" playmates are indeed only imaginary—and that to continue to insist that they actually exist after a certain age would constitute some form of retarded development or mental illness. Of course, some of their playmates may truly be just "made up" by the child. Yet, as a clairvoyant, I have seen that most of children's so-called imaginary playmates are real spiritual beings, just like you and me, except that they do not possess physical bodies as we do.

Just as you know you exist, whether I see you or not, so too a spiritual being can exist without a physical form, whether you see it or not. A spiritual being without a body has its own distinct energy and consciousness just as we do. A psychic child can see, hear, sense, and/or feel the presence of such beings. Some children will be more prone to seeing them, whereas others may hear or feel them more readily. Some will experience such a being even more fully than you might experience another physical person.

The only difference between an "imaginary" playmate, a "ghost," and a "monster" in children's awareness is the character and quality of the spiritual being they are experiencing. It would be similar to you describing someone you like as a "friend," someone you never met before who is behaving strangely as "crazy" or "weird" and classifying a person who looks menacing as "unfriendly" or a "thug."

Psychic children's "imaginary" friends are generally their guardian angels, spirit guides, the spirit of loved ones coming to visit them after their physical deaths, and other friends they have in the spirit world. Ghosts can be spiritual beings who are often so attached psychologically to a place, person, or situation from their last incarnation that they still "hang out" there trying to complete something. Such beings usually don't tend to have anything personally to do with the child who is witnessing their presence. Sometimes they came with the house or place. Often they are attracted to the radiance of the psychic child's light of awareness. At other times, they are seeking help. And, just as we tend to look for a friendly face or a known authority when we are lost in a new town, so too these beings seek out the brighter and kinder among us from whom to try to get communication and help.

There are spiritual beings also that are from other places besides this earth. Of course, we are not alone in this vast universe. And they may or may not look human. Even we may describe some of them as "monsters" if we were to encounter them unprepared and judge them solely by their looks. It isn't surprising that a psychic child, upon seeing such a being, may talk about the "monster in my room." At other times, a psychic child may describe as a "monster" a human spirit who happened to be mean and threatening.

When working with a psychic child, the important thing for you to remember is that you don't just brush her experience off, regardless of the type of being that she identifies. Be willing to learn to work with psychic children and their experience of spiritual beings that you may not see, hear, or feel. Set aside your preconceptions, judgments, and fears. Lighten up and make it fun for both of you to explore and discover a whole new frontier of experience together. Set up a safe space to communicate, and know that the greatest danger is remaining ignorant and refusing to grow.

Working with a Psychic Child's Spirit Friends

As adults, we tend to take enormous responsibility over the welfare of children. It doesn't, however, pay to do so blindly and out of fear. We need to be willing to explore with our psychic children and be open to learning ourselves. Being responsible for a child's well being doesn't mean that we must be on top of everything, know everything, and do everything right. Guiding of the souls of psychic children has less to do with what we know or do and much more to do with how we go about relating to them. Remember that psychic children are *psychic.* What they sense about where you're coming from is often more important to them than what you know or what you can do. Be truthful, happy, and loving with yourself ... and they will know it, feel it, and be more open to you.

Think of working with psychic children and their spirit friends as a learning experience for you, as well. You're going to learn and grow together. You don't always have to be the teacher just because you're the adult; let the children open your heart and mind to new experiences. And learning to work with their spirit friends is a great way to do so.

Even if you don't see or hear spirit guides, angels, or the spirits of deceased loved ones; you can still be a guide to a psychic child who does. Just as a competent TV host guides her guest with good questions to bring out the kind of information and create the quality of experience she wants her audience to have, you can also guide the child toward validation, healing, and growth with simple and honest questions. On a talk show, usually the guest is the expert on the subject and the host may not have a clue about it herself. But she is the one who can make the difference between the show being exciting, educational, and fun ... or a flop. Learn to be a good host and interviewer to your "expert" psychic guest.

Being a good host first means putting the guest at ease. In the case of working with a psychic child, let him feel at home, welcome, and safe. Let him feel that you are sincere and that what he has to say will be heard with respect. But don't be too serious; decide you can have fun with this. In an interview, as with most things in life, humor relaxes and opens a person up. This is especially true with children for, until we grow up, everything is play. Little children always *play* with things. Adults are the ones that *work* at everything.

A great interviewer also engages the guest in conversation: "I'm interested in finding out about your experience. Let's talk about this." Don't talk *at* or *down to* the child, but let him know you're both in this together. An accomplished interviewer knows that she isn't the expert, and that she's the one who wants to learn something new from the guest. Be a good listener and want to find out what the child is going to teach you about his experience.

Finally, don't over do it. Children don't usually give dissertations. Keep it short and sweet. Many bite-sized talks are better than one lengthy one. There's almost always a chance for a follow-up segment.

As for the guiding questions, here are some icebreakers:

- I noticed you were talking with your spirit friend. Was it fun?
- Who is your spirit friend? What do you call him? Does he have a name?
- Do you have many spirit friends?
- Is your spirit friend here with you all the time or do you have to call on him to come talk with you?
- What kinds of things do you talk about or do with your spirit friend?
- Is your spirit friend nice to you?
- Have you known your spirit friend for a long time? How long have you known him?
- What are the things you like about your spirit friend?
- Is there anything you don't like about him?

Once you start to get to know the child's spirit friends and helpers, then you can start to work with the child in enlisting the assistance he or she needs. For example, if the child is having difficulties with schoolwork, a relationship, or wants to hone her ice-skating skills, suggest that she ask her spirit friends to give her some help. You can also think up fun things that she can learn to do with the assistance of her angels, guides, and friends such as asking them to help the two of you get a parking place, help keep the airplane flight safe and stable, or help find a lost object. As with anything else, the more you practice, the better you get at it. Practicing in fun little ways will help lead you and the child to be able to enlist spiritual guidance and assistance in major life changes and healing.

How you handle psychic children's spirit friends, angels, and guides in general would not be much different than how you would manage their relationships with physical friends, caretakers, and teachers. After getting to know them first hand or through the child's experience with them, you would determine what kind of person the friend, caretaker, or teacher is and how healthy their relationship is. For example, even if the teacher is a great person, the way the child is relating to him or her may not be healthy; she may be giving up too much of her power and autonomy to her friend or teacher. Then, that has to be addressed. This may be more about her need to learn to maintain her own seniority and free will than about the other person. At other times, the person may be a definitely negative influence and the child might need to learn to relinquish her attachment to that person. Much of your work with psychic children with regard to their spirit friends would be in empowering them in their natural intuitive ability to know what is true for them and that they have the free will and power within them to manage all their spiritual relationships.

As psychic children grow older and encounter more skepticism and peer pressure, continue to work with them in small but frequent doses. Communicate with them about how people are often afraid to accept the reality of spiritual and psychic matters because they don't feel they have any control over them. Let them know that sometimes it's best not to force the issue and talk about certain things with people who don't believe in them. Yet, let these people know also that it's important that they develop their own certainty in these matters and strengthen their psychic connection within. Reassure them that you are not only available, but are looking forward to talk with them about these matters.

Share books, videos, seminars, and radio and TV shows that validate spiritual guidance and that offer different people's experiences with it. Introduce them to people who are psychic, who have certainty in their spiritual awareness, and are compassionate. Let them know and experience that there are many people who are like them.

What to Do with the Ghosts and Monsters

In the preceding section, we covered some of the basics of approaching a psychic child's encounters with non-physical beings. In the case of questionable and possibly harmful beings, there are further steps you can take.

First, it is important to teach psychic children to be senior to any spirit. Let them learn that they have free will and that, although at times they may not be able to control the circumstances, they always have the choice on how they wish to respond to what is happening. And, that how they choose to respond will invariably have a major effect on the person or the situation. Teach them also that a spiritual being can only have as much power over you as you give to it; that no one can force you to be or do anything against your will.

All that applies to relating with people as well as with other creatures, such as dogs and cats, applies here in one's relationship to non-physical beings. If, for instance, a child came to you and said, "There's a black widow spider in my bedroom," you would not hesitate to go investigate. Just because you can't seem to find it in the room doesn't preclude you from being on the alert and instructing your child to let you know right away if he sees it again. You would take all precautions to ensure that the creature was out of the child's home and you would safeguard his home against future invasion. Of course, doing this in fear and hysteria would diminish your effectiveness. Instead, having neutrality, certainty, compassion, and a touch of humor would be the order of the day.

Likewise, if a psychic child encounters beings that are not beneficent or those that frighten him, investigate thoroughly. If you're not yet capable of psychically experiencing such beings, follow the guidelines set in the previous section for interviewing the child and gathering information. Ask the child, How do you see the ghost / monster / spirit? Where is it? When does it appear to you? Does it do anything? What do you think it wants? What do you think should be done about it?"

Reassure the child and remind him to have his seniority. Let him know that being afraid is normal, but that with more understanding, he will find there is nothing to be afraid of. Explain to him that, as with most wild creatures, they act the way they do because they are afraid of you, too.

What can you do to help remove the unwanted being out of the child's immediate environment? Here your imagination plays a major role. When you imagine something in the present, here and now, you make it real. First, imagine that you can see the being right now. It doesn't matter where it is physically. Imagine that you are totally senior to it and that you are grounding it to the center of the earth with a giant redwood tree, post, or anything that you feel is strong and conductive. This will help stabilize and center the being. Sometimes this alone helps release the being from where it is stuck. If it doesn't, ask the Supreme Being or God for assistance in this. Imagine that you are bringing down a channel of energy right into the top (head) of this being from God. Then, ask God to take this being.

Once you finish with that, decide to reclaim the room and/or the house. Have the child do this with you. Imagine what color of energy would be most suitable for this room (if it is the child's room, let him choose his own color). Imagine that you are setting the energy of this room at that color vibration. Choose the quality of energy you wish the room to be set at—calmness, enjoyment, happiness, or whatever you and the child feel most appropriate. Re-setting the energy of the room daily would be especially helpful.

At the least, this will improve the situation and may even take care of it completely. In the case of an exceptionally persistent or malevolent being, however, the situation would be similar to having a rabid dog or suspicious person on your property; you would call appropriate authorities that are better equipped to handle the situation. Until you are knowledgeable enough to manage it yourself, call on someone who is more experienced in these matters. There are highly competent psychics and spiritual healers who know how to work with such beings. So, who ya gonna call? Ghostbusters!

School and the Psychic Child

Unfortunately, with few exceptions, our schools have generally been set up to foster intellectualism and physicality, and they provide scant breathing room for spirit. I have yet to meet a highly psychic child, even one who fares extremely well academically, who has not suffered the privations of their spirit, with the resulting loneliness, frustration, and sense of futility.

Over the years of my practice, parents have often brought me their psychic children when they were having trouble at school. "Johnny" was one of them. When his mother brought him to see me, he was an eight-year-old who, for reasons no one seemed to be able to determine, could not manage in school. I saw, however, he was one of the brightest souls I'd ever seen. Highly sensitive and remarkably bright, Johnny was so capable that he probably could do anything well given half a chance. Yet, he was on the verge of being extradited from school to some form of institution!

"There's nothing wrong with you," I said to him.

"See, Mom," he squealed, "I *told* you there's nothing wrong with me!"

His mother looked at me in desperation. "But, he's not handling school at all. Not academically, not socially, not in any way," she said.

I explained to Johnny's mom that he was actually too bright and too psychic for most everyone else at his school—his classmates, his teachers, and especially his principal. They could neither understand nor appreciate the extent of his awareness and intelligence. In fact, some of them, particularly the principal, were in competition with him because they could not feel "in control" around him. His mother was floored. She had been told he suffers from severe learning and emotional disabilities. She especially had difficulty fathoming how the principal of the school, who had never even met Johnny, could have such an impact on him. But Johnny immediately responded by exclaiming, "See, Mom, I *told* you that the principal didn't like me!" And his mother later recounted that Johnny *had* been complaining about the principal not liking him for some time. Now, she was more perplexed than ever.

Johnny, on the other hand, was jubilant. He finally had someone who could confirm what he had known all along. He didn't need any drastic healing that his mother had been expecting—he just needed a little validation. His mother, however, needed much more understanding of what was going on.

I worked on the psychic relationship between Johnny and the school principal and healed some of the unconscious antagonism that the principal carried against Johnny. Within a month of the healing, I received a joyful thank you card from Johnny and his mom. They said that he had just been awarded the "Most Improved Student of the Year" honors. Soon, I was receiving cards from them regularly and each one announced another milestone achievement in Johnny's school career: He was elected class president; he was voted "most popular student"; he became the captain of the soccer team; he received the highest grades in his class. And this was the formerly "learning disabled," "socially inept," and "emotionally challenged" outcast in the school. For a soul as psychically connected and capable as this one, all it took was for one person to recognize and validate him as the spirit that he was.

Often, the more psychic the child is, the more misunderstood he may be by parents, teachers, and especially by those who put themselves in positions of authority to control and dominate others, as was the case with Johnny. Highly psychic children are much harder to control by force of will because they know too much, they are able to discern the truth of what someone is telling them, they are often more possessive of their right to be free, and they are more energetic. And these qualities threaten such authoritative personalities who may resort to using their positions of power to try to squelch those very strengths in psychic children.

Psychic Children and UFOs

Exceptionally psychic children often have close encounters with extraterrestrial visitors. I have had encounters with people from other places in the universe throughout my life, so it was not surprising when my younger son, Nick, had a visit when he was eight years old.

I was downstairs in the living room watching a video while Raphaelle, my wife, napped next to me on the couch. Nick and his older brother, Greg, were also fast asleep in their respective bedrooms upstairs. That particular night, for some reason, every single light in the house was off. The only source of illumination was the glow from the TV screen. Our second floor was a partial floor open to the living room area below and I could see Nick's bedroom door from where I was sitting. He had it partially open as he always did.

While I was watching the video I caught a bright flash in the corner of my eye and I heard in my head, "They're here." The hair on the back of my neck stood up and I turned my head up in the direction of Nick's room. In the pitch black of the house, in between the partially open door and the doorframe I saw a brilliant, laser clear blue light. It was one of the most beautiful lights I had ever seen but, oddly, none of it spilled out of Nick's room into the hallway! The light sharply and distinctly ended right at the edge of the doorframe. And the light cast no shadows, either. It was completely contained within Nick's room.

Within a second or two of me taking this scene in, Raphaelle bolted upright from her sleep and grabbed my right arm in a vice-grip and yelled out, "What just happened?" When I turned to face her, she was looking over my shoulder upward toward Nick's room. Then, she said, "Nick, are you okay?"

I turned back around to look upstairs and saw Nick standing staring up to the ceiling while he held onto the railing along the open hallway. He wasn't responding to Raphaelle. Here it goes, I thought to myself and headed up toward his room, stopping to pick up a glass of water for him along the way. But in the few seconds it took me to get up to his room, he was already sound asleep in his bed once again. I noticed that the energy in his room was crisp and smelled mountain fresh—ozone-like after a thunderstorm. I gently woke him up and asked if he was all right.

"Uh-huh," he replied sleepily.

"Did you have any dreams or anything?" I asked him.

"I don't think so," he said.

"Would you like a drink of water?" I offered.

"Sure," he said and sat up to take the glass. "Thanks," he said and fell back to sleep.

The next morning Nick was up early, bright-eyed and full of enthusiasm. I knew he had received some sort of healing from the visitors. "Have any interesting dreams?" I asked him. He replied that he didn't remember any. Then, he said, "You came into my room last night and woke me up." Then, he repeated back to me the whole dialogue we had had word-for-word. "Why did you do that?" he asked.

I explained to him that we had seen him standing staring into what seemed like outer space, unresponsive out in the hallway so I had gone to see if everything was all right. "Really?" he asked incredulous. "That's weird." He had no recall of that part of the scenario. I let it go at that for the time being; I wanted the information to come from him in its own time.

Three months later, I was driving around with Nick and Greg when they started to talk about all the spaceships they saw the two times they went camping on Mt. Shasta with their then step-dad. They described them as lights that went in and out of the mountainside in the middle of the night. Then, out of the blue, Nick announced, "I don't like the people that come in the green light."

Here it comes, I thought. "What people that come in the green light?" I asked.

"The little people," he said.

"Where did you see them?" I continued.

"Oh, at Mom's house. The green light comes into my room while I'm sleeping and then they're there standing in front of my closet."

I asked him, "How many of them visit you and what do they look like?"

He told me, "There are about five of them and they're small and brownish skinned. I don't like them because they sound like they're yelling at me."

I then asked, "If you don't like the ones who come in the green light, are there others you like that come in a different colored light?"

"I don't mind the ones that come in the blue light," he answered. *Pay dirt!*

"Where do they come to you?" I asked.

"Oh, at your house," he answered. "They come into my room there and stand in front of the closet. They're taller and they don't yell at me but talk amongst themselves in a language I can't understand. I think they're talking about me, though. I don't think they ever do anything to me and just leave after a while."

And that was where it stood for the next eleven years. Then, while Nick was practicing his chi gong standing meditation, he said that in a flash of revelation he remembered the whole experience he had had with the extraterrestrial visitors who came in the blue light that night eleven years earlier. He described them coming into his room in the blue light and taking him up to a place made of energy. He said that he was shown on a screen-like space many vivid images of possible future events on earth. He felt he had received much communication and information about what faced humanity and the choices that humanity had to make. The essence of the choice, the visitors had told him, was between living from fear or with love.

Nick recalled that one of the signs that we would see in the world if humanity leans toward living with love was that dolphins and whales will show themselves to and interact more and more with people. On the other hand, if humanity chooses to stay in fear, he said, the dolphins and whales would start to beach themselves and die off. (It is interesting to note also that highly psychic children are especially fond of and attract dolphins.)

Nick recalled being shown so many scenes of possible wars and suffering if humanity doesn't make the correct choices. He also remembered scenes of cataclysmic earth changes but felt that all things would come to pass ultimately for the good. One of the visions that particularly struck him was that of the earth stopping its rotation and gravity being absent for a time. He saw some people floating up into the sky as well as the stars in the sky appearing to fall. He felt that knowing how to ground oneself and be centered was going to be crucial during such a time.

As to him standing in the hallway outside his room that night, Nick recalled that he didn't walk out to the hallway, but was returned there after his visit in what he realized was a spaceship.

I know he had truly experienced all of this because I had nearly the same experience shortly after Nick had his, except in my case, the visitors approached me while I was awake and fully conscious, and I remained conscious throughout my whole experience. All of what he was shown, I, too, was shown. And I had never communicated to him what I was shown by the extraterrestrial visitors.

An interesting sidelight of Nick's experience was that within the two weeks following his initial encounter, I had met many panicked parents about their children being visited by extraterrestrial people in UFOs at that time. Many of them reported seeing the same brilliant blue light in their children's room.

As for Nick, he recently told me, "All my life so far has been preparation for the times that are soon coming. I wouldn't have missed this lifetime for anything."

I have always felt the same way.

Picking up Other People's Thoughts, Emotions, and Problems

Close encounters with a variety of beings are not all that occupy a psychic child's development. In fact, one of the most common challenges for most psychic children is learning to discern whether their feelings and thoughts are really their own. They need to ask themselves, "Are these thoughts that I'm thinking mine? Could the emotions I'm feeling belong to someone else?"

We are all high-powered broadcasting and receiving stations for all kinds of energetic signals. We not only send out, but also pick up thought and emotional vibrations. We work like TV sets and radios, picking up different broadcasts at different frequencies. We can tune into other people's thoughts and emotions as well as our own inner signals.

Children who are sensitive to psychic energy can easily feel their parents' unexpressed emotions, their teacher's unspoken criticism, or their best friend's hidden desires. Most naturally assume that the desires and emotions they feel are their own. Unknowingly they may struggle with academic or personal problems seeping into their awareness from their classmates. Those psychic children who are also healers may have a particularly difficult time because of their desire to help others.

Most of the children with learning difficulties that I work with have no problems with their intelligence or capacity to learn. They are simply overwhelmed with all the psychic broadcasts they pick up from classmates, teachers, and families. And they can't focus their attention on their class assignments. Once they learn to ground out the excess energy, discern their own thoughts and feelings, and define their psychic space, they are able to learn exceptionally well.

Not knowing this at the time, I struggled through my elementary school years. Because I cared far more about the troubled souls around me than my studies, I would have my attention psychically wrapped up in their problems. Without any validation of my psychic experience, I ended up trying to solve them as my own problems and often spun my wheels. It took me much longer to learn my assignments and I frequently got sick from all the problems I carried in me.

If you catch children early enough, they'll be able to tell you how others are feeling or what others may be thinking. But once they've begun to lose that psychic connection, they need to be reminded first that, at times, they can be picking up on other people's thoughts and emotions.

It is also important for them to learn that they cannot control how someone else feels or thinks. So, when they become aware that they are tuning into what someone else is thinking or feeling, they must not take personal responsibility for trying to change or fix it. If they can learn to let the other person first think and feel as they do, then they will not take on the other's problems. Being free of those problems, the healer would then be able to respond to that person in a way that would help them change for the better.

A simple rule of thumb in determining whose energies you're dealing with is whether you can solve it, change it, or stop it. If you can't, it's not yours. For example, if the child is picking up his sister's anger, as long as he is tuned into her and she remains angry, he'll continue to feel that anger, whether he wants to be angry or not. No matter how much he tries to solve "his" anger problem, he'll be unable to do so. However, once he realizes that the anger he is feeling isn't his, he can decide to let go of trying to stop it or solve it. He can then be taught to redirect his attention to how his own inner energy feels and, even if his sister is still furious, he'll feel a lot better! I call this, "changing the channel." If we change whom we're tuning into as well as the frequency we're tuning into, we can feel and think completely differently, as when you change the channel on your TV; you get an entirely different program.

Remembering Dreams and Out-of-Body Experiences

From a spiritual perspective, our dreamtime is just as important as our waking hours, for it is during sleep that we take time off from the rigors of worldly existence and return temporarily to our heavenly home. We can also use our dreamtime for an extraordinary amount of learning, healing, and growth.

Psychic children are especially aware of their out-of-body experiences, including what they experience during their sleep. Many return to their bodies regularly with their memory of those experiences intact. For the majority of adults, however, even though they may get out of their bodies just as much, their mental "filters" have gotten clogged and they don't recall as much. Some might even assume that nothing happens at all while they slumber.

Others, such as Raphaelle, have continued into adulthood clearly remembering their dreamtime experiences. She told me about a particularly prophetic and enlightening dream she first had when she was five years old. Every time her connection to her spiritual purpose started to fade in her life, this dream would recur.

In the dream, she sits in the back of a boat behind her parents and oldest brother in a lake facing a formidable mountain in the distance. A guide's voice explains that this scene represents the early portion of her life in which she was to work out past issues (karma) with her parents and oldest brother. Her immediate environment seems bleak, but he also points out that behind the mountain, where she can see a hint of a radiant sunrise, she will discover the fulfilling life as the spiritual teacher she was born to be. To climb that mountain and reach her fulfillment, however, he shows her she will need a chisel, a hammer, and a variety of other tools. These, he explains, are *spiritual* tools that she will need to learn in order to accomplish her task. And throughout the dream, the guide repeats to her, "Remember this: You have lived many times before and you will live again." Each time she has this dream, Raphaelle says she awakens with a renewed sense of her spiritual self and purpose.

Many psychic children are avid dreamtime explorers. Some report dreams of a symbolic nature in which they work out current life challenges, while others experience prophetic dreams or dreams in which they work on skills such as in sports, music, or academics. Often a psychic child may pursue healing himself or others during the dream state.

One time when my older son, Greg, was thirteen, he went to sleep concerned about his friend who was quite sick and therefore he couldn't visit. He soon found himself floating out of his body and traveling down the hall into my bedroom. Hovering above my sleeping body, he experienced talking to me about wanting to go give healing to his sick friend. Then, he saw me float out of my body to join him and the two of us went flying to his friend's house to give him healing. The next day, Greg discovered upon calling him, that his friend had suddenly got well overnight and that Greg could go visit him!

When working with psychic children, it is important to regularly discuss their dreamtime remembrances with them. You can also make it a fun way to validate their spiritual out-of-the-body experiences and learning. The more they receive validation of their out-of-the-body experiences, the more they will be able to remember who they are as spirit and be present in their bodies during their "waking" hours.

Mediumship

A soul enters and exits a physical body through the avenue and ability called "mediumship." Those who possess a greater capacity for mediumship can more fully experience and express their higher spiritual potentials and are known as "mediums." Since mediumship is the conduit for spirit to go in and out of a body, not only the originally incarnated soul but also other beings can channel through the medium as well. This can cause some psychic children who are such open channels to be highly affected by other spirits unless they learn to properly manage this powerful ability.

Common signs exhibited by children struggling with their mediumship ability can range from hyperactivity, "bouncing off the walls," difficulties focusing, frequently "spacing out," extreme shyness, or regularly saying and doing things "they didn't mean to." Highly mediumistic children can be hypersensitive to other people's psychic energies and, combined with the ease with which they exit their bodies, they end up leaving themselves vulnerable to channeling energies other than their own. This may mean that they are "gone" and no one's home in their body or that some other being enters their body and they become a stranger to you.

You may have known people who act as if they are two or more different people depending on when you talk to them. A person may clearly and coherently discuss something with you one moment and later sincerely deny ever doing so. A person you've known intimately can sometimes turn into a complete stranger. Who are you really with?

When this aspect of mediumship affects a psychic child and he doesn't have any validation of what's going on with him spiritually, he may become afraid and ashamed and try to hide it or deny it. For the sensitive soul, to be accused of things he has never done can be a terrifying experience. All the physical evidence "proves" he has, only he may not have been the one who was in his body when the act occurred!

Imagine what it would be like for you if you passed out and, upon "coming to," you are blamed by those around you for terrible things you did while you were unconscious. You have no memory of it and you wouldn't do such a thing. Yet everyone else is convinced you did. It's often like that for a child whose mediumship is out of control.

This mediumship ability can turn on especially in psychic teenagers. The intense hormonal changes, combined with all the mental and emotional challenges that accompany the teen years, can make the sensitive soul want to abandon its body. Once again, when the soul isn't fully present, the body can become an open channel for foreign energies to come through it. Often, however, it isn't other entities that "possess" one's body but other people's energies and desires that channel through it. This could also result in teens saying and doing things they didn't really intend and later regret—"It just happened." Or, they could fall totally in love with a person one day and wake up the next morning asking, "What got into me?"

One of the great dangers also for teens and young adults with a high degree of uncontrolled mediumship is falling into alcoholism or drug abuse. The consumption of alcohol or drugs enables the soul to readily abandon its body by "loosening the circuits" that normally keep it tethered. Once humanity discovered it, troubled souls have regularly sought out a drink or ten for the temporary relief of vacating their pain-filled bodies.

Alcoholics particularly tend to deny their alcoholism since the original incarnated soul may only experience the first drink or two. He then takes off and other beings enter his body to do the rest of the drinking. When the original being finally returns, he may be telling the truth that, "I only had a couple of drinks."

In whatever manner psychic children manifest their uncontrolled mediumship, to begin to heal themselves they first need validation of their spirituality and psychic experience: They are spiritual beings and they are psychic. Talk to the spiritual beings that they are. Learn to use your intuition to experience the true spirit of the child.

Communication is energy and your energy moves according to your intent. Know that, when you are clear in your intent, whatever you are saying will reach the spirit of that child whether that soul is present in its body or out of it. Trust your intuition to know whether the correct being is in that child's body. Don't verbally wrestle with the occupant if it isn't the original owner. Intend that your verbal or telepathic communication will find the soul with whom you would like to talk. Let the true spirit of the child feel your sincere desire to be with him and to talk with him—and let him know that you're not interested in being with the intruder. Do not give any seniority to the being that has taken over. Instruct the original soul that for his own well being, he needs to return to his body. All healing begins with the soul being present in its body here and now.

Restoring the Psychic Connection

Few of us growing up as psychic children survive these psychic challenges unscathed. Yet the truth of the matter is that healing and growth are always possible. For psychic children growing into adulthood, the late teens and early twenties are crucial times to begin restoring their psychic connection. All they need is their willingness to turn inward to truth and the limitless loving nature of Divinity to start that process. Foster in them a sense of trust and certainty that, when they are ready and willing to learn and grow, the teachers and the healers always appear. Teach them also that teachers and healers come in all manner of guises, so they had better shed any fixed expectations.

Especially with teens, one of the best ways to start them on healing their psychic connection is by applying their learning and practice of psychic tools and spiritual truths to whatever specific practical interests they may have. For example, when my son Nick was seventeen and preparing for his second boxing tournament, he realized that he didn't have a problem with being physically trained and prepared to fight his opponent. His trepidation focused instead on handling the enormous psychic pressure he felt from the crowd during his previous fight.

He asked me if there were any psychic tools that could give him the edge in managing all of the energy that surrounded the fight.

We worked on incorporating psychic tools and spiritual awareness into his daily training regimen. Nick successfully applied them and was able to not only manage the fight but to win. As a result of his success, Nick regained his enthusiasm for restoring more of his psychic connection that had faded somewhat in his early teens.

I've also worked many times with young women who were most interested in having a good romantic relationship with a man. Some of these women would otherwise not have been interested in psychic awareness or their spirituality. When they realized, however, that most of their relationship problems with men had to do with their mismanagement of their psychic abilities and energies, then their interest in learning to reconnect with their inner being became paramount.

Often psychic children, especially teens, are struggling to regain a sense of meaning and purpose in their young lives. The question, "What are you going to become when you grow up?" echoes in their mind. Indeed, they discover that they *are* growing up. But have they *become* anything meaningful, important, or great yet? The expectations of parents, teachers, coaches, ministers, and friends—from TV and Hollywood, too—haunt many of them daily.

When I was growing up, adults invariably asked me, "What are you going to be when you grow up?" I thought, *What's wrong with what I am now?* I felt that who, what, and how I was was unacceptable, and that I had to grow up into something more important, more valuable. Also, there was little validation that what you were eventually going to become was already inside of you. The focus was on going out there to somehow get it, "You go out there and get an education, get a degree, get a job, find a career."

When you're asked what you're going to become when you grow up, you can either feel you know the answer or you can be scared of growing up. Some psychic children try to grow up fast, act the part of adults, and be really "together." Meanwhile, others avoid growing up as long as possible so that they won't be caught grown up and not having become anything "worthwhile."

As children, we often make up something just so that we can have a sense of purpose, some meaning in our life: "I'm going to be a doctor." *Ah, that's a good thing.* Your parents calm down, people are proud of you, and now you're acceptable because you're going to become somebody. So, that's what I told everyone from the time I was seven years old. That is, until I found myself in college majoring in pre-med and started asking myself: *Wait a minute, what am I doing here?* And I began my intensive search to recover my psychic connection.

Psychic children employ various means to try to keep the embers of their spiritual life alive until they can find the permission, opportunity, and tools to fully restore their psychic connection. My teacher had people show up in his life who would restore his trust in his inner awareness when it began to wane. Raphaelle found that her childhood dream and guidance revisited her at crucial junctures every time she strayed off her path. Nick has told me that whenever he feels hopelessly lost he returns to a place of golden light and infinite love that he remembers from before his birth. Know that every exceptionally psychic child has his or her own way of keeping the connection alive. Through our relationship with them, we must learn their secrets and together we can move toward our full healing and restoration of divinity.

Super Psychic Children and the Future of Humanity

The more each of us begins to restore our psychic connection and become spiritually aware, the more permission and validation we create in the world for souls to incarnate with even more of their psychic freedom, awareness, and abilities. Over the course of the past 30 years, I have seen an exponential rise in the number and power of exceptionally psychic children. More and more of them are demonstrating extraordinary capabilities and wisdom even amongst psychics.

I have known children who could mentally (telekinetically) throw couches and chests of drawers across the room without ever physically touching them. I have seen little kids tip over solid oak tables from across the room with their mind. I've worked with children who materialized bags of cookies literally from thin air because the chaperones forgot to buy them at the store for their birthday party! I was given a photo taken of a child engrossed in levitating a sock in mid-air during childcare. I know many children who have teleported lost objects back to their owners. Several of my adult friends who are currently extraordinary healers and psychics were the early super psychic children who had been institutionalized for being able to do things that no one understood or was willing to understand. But now, I am teaching more and more adults to regain the psychic connections that they had as children but lost them in their childhood battle of invalidation.

Today, more and more "super-psychic" children are being "discovered" around the world. There are those who retain photographic knowledge of whole books just by putting them under their armpits or feet; those who can command seeds to sprout right on the palm of their hand; those who can teleport objects through time and space; and even those who can literally walk through solid walls. These super psychic children are the heralding angels of a new and evolving humanity. They are now arriving to live amongst us and demonstrate the next steps in the potentials of human consciousness. Bending forks and spoons may not in themselves serve any practical purpose in our lives, but they serve to teach us to re-examine the limits of our commonly held beliefs. Gravity, though it may affect most of us, does not rule supreme for spirit.

Even more important than the ability to levitate or teleport, however, is the power to heal. Although healers have always been here throughout history to help with the evolvement of humanity, today, unprecedented numbers of psychic children are reincarnating as healers. These extraordinary healers are changing the world by making the exceptional capabilities they possess "normal" for the general population to develop. The entire practice of medicine will eventually become advanced temporary first-aid measures for those of us who have yet to master healing ourselves. In my heart of hearts, I know that disease would become all but obsolete through the loving power of the spirit.

The Bible tells us that the children shall lead us into a new way of life. That time has come. It is now up to us as adults to bring about the necessary changes in the way we raise our psychic children: how we feed, clothe, and educate not only their physical bodies and minds but their psychic being, their souls, as well. The future of humanity and our world rests upon the choices we make in nourishing and nurturing the soul of our psychic children.

A preeminent spiritual visionary, Michael Tamura is world-renowned for his profound wisdom as a spiritual teacher, healer and clairvoyant. For almost three decades he has been guiding the souls of thousands of men, women and children through his powerful class teachings and client sessions. In addition to his on-going private practice, Michael conducts spiritual self-healing seminars, lectures and retreats throughout the US and abroad.

With over twenty-nine years of experience as a spiritual teacher and healer, Michael recently reached a milestone in his career with the release of his inspirational first book You Are the Answer: An Extraordinary Guide to Entering the Sacred Dance with Life and Fulfilling Your Soul Purpose. *Visit his website >www.michaeltamura.com< or contact him via e-mail >tamuras@ix.netcom.com<.*

72.

Your children already know the way to the truth we are describing.
The key is to help them "not forget."
You once knew it too,
But the unreal world claimed your attention.
Now you have the chance to heal this wound
By guarding them.

73.

The tree is now mature and the fruit is ripe.
It will fall from the branch by itself.
You don't need to shake it.

You have made the roots strong.
Give yourself credit for this.

74.

Try not to focus on what you have to do,
But rather on what has already been done.

This is the key for raising any child,
Including yourself.

75.

Here is the most important thing I can teach you:
There is a child alive within you now
Who has everything it needs to be happy.
There is nothing you need that is not already present.
This is the key to your salvation.

When you realize this,
Then your children will realize the same.
That is why I keep telling you that you don't
Need to worry about your children.
You don't need to worry about anything.

76.

When the sun rises it will be easy
For you to open your eyes.
You have been trying to wake up
While it is still dark outside.
Most people will only fall back to sleep.
But now everything is different.

The sun is shining.

77.

Birds don't need to learn how to fly.
They open up their wings and allow the wind to claim them.
Your children will react the same
If you show them how to open their souls.

How do you do this?
You already know the answer.

78.

There may come times when your children are afraid
To open their wings and fly.
You may need to give them a gentle push.
It's the only way they will realize they are ready.

The best way to push them is by setting a good example.

79.

If you want to understand how the children are working
together
To heal the world,
Watch a flock of migrating geese.
They fly together and take turns leading the rest.

80.

Test the sky and realize that you are at home there.
Open your eyes and know that
Your feet have never touched the ground.
You were made for flight
Though you have never believed it was true.

Appendix

1. Isaac and the Dream of Heaven

By Libby Maxey

Isaac Andrew is my exuberant six-year-old. He is a child of joy. Before he was born, his spirit would come to me as a handsome, strong, young man with a cheeky smile that could melt glaciers, clothed in golden light. God called him a "Joshua" spirit, though I had no idea what that might mean. My beloved teacher, Ernestine, told me he was coming as the protector of my spirit. He does keep me in Love, that's for sure. He has often surprised and amazed me with his deeply simple spiritual insight and we frequently speak the same thoughts. One astounding night we dreamt the same dream.

This dream was truly a vision—vivid and real. I fear this dream; I am in awe of it as well. It began with my family gathered at a vacation place. We were attending some sort of a reunion being held at a beautiful outdoor park. Isaac excitedly grabbed my hand, pulling me, wanting me to come down to the water with him. We ran together to a rocky area, to a large irregular pool of sparkling, clear water. It seemed to be a spring-fed pond, the clarity of the water indicating constant movement. The water was surrounded by rock walls of layered stone, perhaps a state park in Tennessee or Kentucky. One of the rock walls formed a shaded cave-like area in the water; Isaac was particularly attracted to that spot. I watched from above as he descended some old man-made concrete steps into the water. He splashed and played in the cool water, then asked if he could climb the rocks. Knowing the futility of telling a young boy "no," I said "yes," but only where I could see him. The place I pointed out looked safe, like stair steps. Isaac climbed nimbly up, and down, back and forth.

He came to where I sat, asking me to come down in the water and watch him climb another wall, a more jagged-looking part, and steeper. I went with him, laughing at his enthusiasm. The spot was adjacent to the concrete steps, rising perhaps twelve feet above the shallow water. Scampering about as boys do, Isaac took one step too far and down he fell, slow motion, into the shallow, clear water, down between the concrete steps and the rock wall, down in the water shaded by both. I could not see him in the shaded darkness, but only heard his earlier laughter as it echoed off the rocks. I raced down the stairs, feeling nothing beneath my feet, glancing over to where I thought he landed, finally catching a glimpse of his blond hair. Without thought I was there, reaching into the water and gathering up his limp little body, cradling his smashed and bleeding head there in the shallow, rocky place.

I knew he was leaving. With the last life left in his little body, he looked at me and smiled, green eyes shining, face glowing. His beautiful cheeky little boy smile, filled with infinite gratitude and eternal love, filled with His Peace. We closed our eyes together, Isaac and I, and I watched as his spirit-form scampered up the rocky wall, up and up, to the top where we could both plainly see the Light of God. At the top was a grassy, flower-strewn plateau, and a form, a beautiful, familiar being appeared, standing with his back to us, about ten feet away.

The luminous Being turned, Isaac shouted "Jesus!" and flinging a last adoring, excited smile over his shoulder at me, ran flying to Jesus, who knelt to catch him in his waiting arms. Jesus looked up at me, smiling that same smile filled with All of Everything, and they merged as one being. The dream ended.

When I awoke suddenly from this dream, I felt different. I felt adrift, as if cut loose from everyone and everything. It was a good feeling, mostly, very liberating, even joyful. I walked around in a daze that day and the next, the dream images haunting every thought. Then three days later, Isaac was particularly quiet when I picked him up after work. We had traveled perhaps a mile when he spoke, with gravity in his voice I had never heard. "Mom, I need to tell you something," he said. I waited, expectant, glancing in the rearview mirror at his little face, so serious. "Okay, sweetie, I'm listening," I said.

"Next time I go to heaven, I'm not coming back." He spoke with confidence, with an air of decided finality, totally unlike a six-year-old. I nearly wrecked the car, the entire dream flooding back into my mind. I knew, I absolutely knew that Isaac and I had participated in a real event, a shared experience only God could provide. "So what made you come back, anyway?" I asked, my voice shaking, hoping he couldn't hear my emotion. "It was you, Mom, I love you and I am here for you. I came back to you. You called to me. But I wanted to stay with Jesus, Mom. He's so beautiful and nice. Everything was so beautiful and nice. Nobody needed anything, everybody was happy all the time. The flowers even smiled, Mom. I love it there, Mom, and next time I'm not coming back. Okay?" Tears streamed down his little face. "Okay, Isaac, next time you stay with Jesus. Can I come, too?" "Oh yes, Mommy, please come with me too. That would be perfect." He sighed with great relief, a burden too big for his six-year-old consciousness lifted.

He sat there in silence for a short while. I regained some small amount of composure, glad that I had the distraction of driving the car, happy there was no traffic. "Tell me about heaven, Isaac," I offered. Eager, he sat forward. "Oh, Mom, it's exactly like I remember. The light feels so good all over. Nobody thinks about what they want or need, everybody has everything all the time. The flowers and trees are alive, Mom, it's like they're little people. They look at you and follow you around there. It's weird, but I like it. There are people and angels everywhere, all around. It's all like, soft, or something. I want to stay there, Mom."

Ahh, little one, the whole world wants to stay there.

Libby Maxey and Isaac reside in Lebanon, Tennessee, with Aaron and Laura – and Kitty the beagle dog, their protector angel with fur.

2. High Thoughts from a Psychic Child

by Paulette Wittman

My son, Christopher, began exhibiting behavior at 18 months that indicated he might remember past lives. Over the next few years he remembered several incidents including deaths. He also exhibited some skill recall, such as having been a concert pianist and orchestra position 1st violin on the Titanic. He remembered that one at age 4.

As soon as Christopher could sit up he began rocking and humming/chanting. After he was weaned from the breast at 20 months, this act would be the first thing he did (and still does) in the morning. Around age 5, when asked why he did this, his answer was "To call back my spirit. It left my body during the night and didn't all come back yet."

Age 5-7 seemed to be a real significant time for him as far as his spiritual recall and expression. He actually levitated during one of his rocking-chanting times. It scared him and has not happened since. At that time he also began expressing thoughts that I could barely comprehend. In my journal I have noted statements such as: "I think all things happen at once—past, present, and future. I am a baby and an old person at the same time. Yesterday, today, and tomorrow are all now."

"I think we are God's daydream. I mean, I think He is just thinking us in His head and that is what creates us. He dreams us." "We are all the same, like fingers. They only think they are separate but they are part of one hand, one arm, one person. Or leaves. They only think they are individual but they are part of a tree. We only think we are individual but we are all part of God—in His mind." "I think we can do anything, we just think we can't." "None of this is really here, you know, it's like we are a dream." "You can only touch it because you think it is hard." "I forgot how to fly. I know I can but being in this body, I forgot how to make it not heavy" "Why can't I just think myself somewhere and be there? We are supposed to be able to do that but I just don't remember how to do it." "Why can't I make this disappear? I am willing it to, it's supposed to." This was all from a small child with no exposure to anything metaphysical, paranormal etc.

Over the next 9 years he seemed to forget all that wisdom and became a regular little boy. Christopher is almost 17 years old now. Over the past year he has begun getting in touch with that part of himself again. He has commented that he remembers his powers and abilities. He states he knows he is a healer and a teacher. He has tried, without any education, to create and manipulate energy. I feel if he had education and guidance he would be extremely powerful. He has stated he feels he has great knowledge just outside his reach. He needs someone to help him to recall that. He has stated many times he feels he is a "master" and asks why it is so hard for him to reclaim his knowledge and ability. He once felt he was in his body backward or sideways. Christopher is teaching himself energy healing. He practices and has had a lot of success.

My grandson, Haven, is another special child. I feel he is a gifted healer, perhaps a "crystal" child. When he was conceived, his mother had Lupus SLE. It's an incurable, potentially fatal disease. When Haven was 2 weeks old, he and his mother had to be checked to see how badly the pregnancy and birth had hurt the mother, and also to see if any of the Lupus had crossed to the baby. There was absolutely no sign of the disease in the mother. She apparently is healed. Haven is almost 3 years old now and it may be my prejudice and imagination, but it seems that just holding him makes people well, especially if they have been emotionally ill, as we don't generally let physically ill people hold him. This child has very high intelligence as well. I look for him to connect to profound wisdom in the way Christopher has.

I believe advice I would give to other parents and grandparents is to be open with children and accept their memories and gifts. Too often parents feel threatened and shame the children, belittle them, and make them feel it is just their imagination. The children then choose to shut it off so as not to appear weird or strange. I, myself, was a strange child. I know how that feels.

Something I did for my son was to teach him to meditate. I bought him a tape set especially for children. He soon graduated to my adult meditation sets and mastership training programs.

If we accept our children, no matter how odd, different, or strange they seem, it teaches them to accept themselves and others. This also nurtures the gifts they chose to come into this world with, keeping them one more step ahead.

Paulette Wittman, a single parent of three and grandmother of one, works in home health and hospice in Kansas and is a full time nursing student along with being a student of Reiki and Healing Touch. Paulette also has had past life recall, mediumistic, and healing abilities since childhood. Contact Paulette at >paulette@empathi.com<.

3. Little Buddhas

by Arlene Riddick

When I began the Psychic Children Course a few months ago (offered through >emissaryoflight.com<), my first experience of their message was very profound. I had gone into a meditation, and I had accessed that state of being that seems to be outside of us ... that something "bigger than us." I saw myself on my deathbed, a very old woman. My two girls, Abigail and Grace, were grown, and they were at my side, each holding my hands. The love that I felt for them was immense, and it was complete. But what struck me the most was that, within my meditation, I was flashing back over my life. And what I saw and felt was that I had had a wonderful life with my children ... we had loved each other greatly. It was this that I was taking with me to the other side—our love for each other—and there was profound peace in that. I came out of that meditation very in touch with what life can be, and I was transformed out of that message.

My name is Arlene, and I am the mother of twelve-year-old Abigail and four-year-old Grace. What can I say to impart to you who they are? They are the lights in my life; they are whom I persevere for in the face of all that life deals me. At times, I feel I could pull my hair out over some of the things they do ... "children" things.

And at other times, things that they say or do bring me to the core of my being and remind me of what I am here to do. They remind me to love—they remind me of who I am, who they are, and who humanity is. They bring me back to God every time I think that I want to run away.

I had a third daughter as well, actually she was my first. Her name was Lise, and she would have been fourteen now. She was born on the first day of spring. My husband and I used to call her "Little Buddha." The spirit shining from within her seemed incredibly wise. She died four and a half months after her birth on August 6, the day of Christ's Transfiguration. She actually died as he did with both arms outspread. I had never been so happy in all my life as I had when I found out that I was pregnant with her. And I had finally turned back to God, because that, of course, is where children lead you. And then I felt she had been ripped from me, and my world as I knew it crumbled beneath me. I felt in a foreign land, and yet I knew that I had to remain in touch with God because my baby was with him. So, I trusted that everything would be all right, and I opened my arms to receive Abigail a year and a half later. I learned to be happy again.

She helped to restore my faith, and taught me to open my heart again and to keep going. God had blessed me a second time. Abigail has a sweetness about her that leaves no doubt who she is. She loves children and animals, she is kind, she is courageous, and she is bright and loving. She is beautiful inside and out. My husband Ted and I seemed to relax a bit under her influence.

And then when Abbey was almost six, Ted, took his life. Again, I felt catapulted into oblivion. But, even more devastating to me, was that Abbey should have to live through such a nightmare. But as God would have it, He would not let me stray again, and He spoke His heart to me through her as we pulled away from my sister's house a day after Ted's death. She said to me, "Mama, I don't care about my toys. I don't care about anything, because love is all there is. And Daddy just needed to learn about love."

Well, it had taken me just about 40 years to learn that one! And she came into this life with that knowing. In that instant, she had put things in a perspective that I had grappled to see all of my life. In my deepest grief, she spoke hope to me. So, I put one foot in front of the other, got us the emotional help that we needed, and worked again on trusting that God had a plan for me and Abbey. Well, He did, because just two and a half years later, Gracie came to us.

She came to make us laugh. That is the energy of Grace. She has a mischievous twinkle in her eyes that makes them sparkle. And she, like Abbey, was sent to me from God to remind me of Him. She told me once when she was three that all there was was just now and now and now and now. I needed to remind myself that she was just a baby. She has recently been telling me that God speaks in her ears, and that it is a funny sound. She told me that God likes to hear her giggle, because He wants her to be happy, and that God has the power, and He is the only one. There is nowhere else that she hears things like this. It makes the hair stand up on the back of my neck.

And so, that is it ... so profound and yet so simple ... so simply pure! To me, my children are here to remind me that "love is all there is."

Arlene Riddick lives in New Orleans, Louisiana.

4. The Button Pusher

by Joycelin Chalmers

How does one raise a child who is psychic, indigo, knowing? First, don't raise them like we were. They really don't need to be raised. They need to be loved. They are different from you and me. They come into this life with more memory of who they are. They are not for us to control through fear or drugs. They have more energy than we possess ... more imagination, more knowing. They have a purpose. We are to be mentors to them, and help them to keep their gifts intact.

They are non-conformists. They will rebel if you or anyone else tries to control them. Remember how you felt when your parents wanted control over you? This is even more. These children are on a mission. They are here to bring more love in. When my son was around four years old we were driving home and he said out of nowhere, "I am here to push buttons."

"What?" I said.

"It's so you know where they are." He's 12 now and still remembers that. I told him the other day not to do the button pushing with certain people. He's done his job and now it is their choice as to whether or not to heal those places. Just love them. He's not sure I am right and frankly neither am I, but he agreed.

I am currently involved in the Junior Church of the Foothill Center of Religious Science. It is a community of people who, like me, know that Spirit is omnipresent. The children are all really special kids. Some remember who they are, some have forgotten. My goal, my aim is to remind them of their ONENESS. What I do know is that teaching, as they do it in most schools, treats kids as if they are empty vessels to be filled, which just insults them and makes them rebellious. They do not learn like other children. They CAN learn in the same way; however, they have more questions—and we are usually baffled by most of them. They use more of their brain, and they learn best through experience.

So, I asked Joshua, because he knows, "How do we get the other kids in Junior Church to ***knowing***?"

First he said, "I don't know."

I rephrased the question. "How do you know that you are one?" I then got a quizzical look.

I had asked him one day last week, "Where is God, the presence, the All That Is?" He looked at me like I was purple. "Please," I said, "just tell me what you know."

"Everywhere," he answered, "in you, in me, in all of everything."

So I ask, "How do you know?"

"You told me, and I believe you."

"Okay," I said, "but, at some point in time you went from believing it, to knowing it. What happened? How did you do that?"

"Meditation, especially that one."

"Which one?" I am feeling excited here.

"The vehicle, the protection, the light speed."

"Oh, I get it, the Merkaba?"

"Yes," he confirms, "that's it."

"What happened?" I asked, as I thought back to 6 years ago. I had gone to a workshop called The Flower of Life, and I learned the meditation Drunvalo Melchizedek taught. I didn't teach him that meditation. I had him sit between my legs, his back to my front and I did the meditation.

"When you did that I felt everything. I just knew I was a part of everything and everything was me. I saw light, I saw a tunnel of light, I didn't die but there was the light."

"Okay," I said, "So, how do we help the others to experience that?"

"Do meditation with them."

"That will do it?"

"Yes. But, Mom, you will have to be the one to do it."

I felt I had been paid a high, high compliment.

So, raise them? That makes me laugh. Allow them to explore who they are.

If they have forgotten, help them to remember their magnificence. Find guided meditations that appeal to them. Ask them about themselves. Share information with them from the workshops you do. Read the books with them about the Indigo Children. Explain and listen to their thoughts on each and every subject. Assist them in finding what their purpose is, what their mission is. Remind them that they know who they are. Really connect with them. Never, ever lie to them. Do not make excuses to them. If you promise them something make sure you keep your word, even if it is a consequence to behavior. Integrity is everything. Learn from them—they are here to teach us, too.

Jocelyn Chalmers' number one priority is Spirit first. It is the Energy throughout all. She works as a holistic health practitioner, an intuitive healer, a Reiki Master/ Teacher, a writer and a mother.

5. Mom of Six

By Hilary Adams

The subject of the special children is very near and dear to my heart for I have six of them. I knew from the minute each of these precious souls emerged from my body (and even during my pregnancy) that each one was sent with their own agenda and life purpose.

When my son, Zack, started school, I was told something was wrong and I should seek the advice of professionals. We did and he was put on medication. The same scenario happened with each of the four oldest who are in school now. The medications did not help at all and the behavior modification the doctors suggested was very time consuming and not very nurturing.

I spent eight years being an advocate for my children in the school district to no avail. Nobody wanted to understand them and moreover they were being ignored, categorized, and pushed from one person to another. They were labeled, ostracized, made fun of, and outcast by their peers. The true essence of their little souls was completely taken away by a society trying to push all their rules and regulations on them. It makes me wonder how they could still be so loving and kind. I just look at them with awe at the light and love coming from them.

During the summer of 2002, my twelve-year-old, Nick, started having conversations with me about the animals and dream premonitions. This is my child who has animals following him home from everywhere. A few years back we had the opportunity to have Nick in a therapeutic horseback riding program where I witnessed him standing in the horse arena among all the horses because they all wanted to be near him. During that summer, Nick told me he talked to the animals and not only did he talk to the animals, they talked to him. During one of our many conversations I asked Nick why he didn't tell me long ago and he said, "Because Mom, I thought you would think I was weird." I felt as if I had somehow failed Nick and began to wonder why he felt like he couldn't share this wonderful part of his life with me.

That same summer I started reading everything I could about the Indigo children. This is where I learned that my children were gifted; then I became a little upset at all of the things people had been telling me were "bad" and "not normal" about my kids, that had now become a blessing. It just rips my heart out to hear all the negative labels given to these children.

I have witnessed many wonderful things since I have opened my heart to them; as my children become more intuitive, I have learned that I grow right alongside them. It always amazes me when a parent of one of these special children says to me "But Johnny just won't listen to me." I then reply, "Are you listening to him?" Why do people think we have to teach our children and talk at them rather than listen and talk with them?

When the medication didn't work, I went in search of another way to help my children and found Karen Curry in Sedona, Arizona. Through her, I learned about Emotional Freedom Technique (EFT) from the EFT web site >www.emofree.com<. I feel empowered by the universe to help my children and myself. I wish I could tell every parent of a special child about EFT and scream it from the mountaintop to stop medicating your children ... listen to them and use the universe to help you.

On a brighter note, my family and I are in a much better place today. However, the school year started with a bang when my first grade Meg's teacher came over to my car filled with my five children and started screaming at me telling me Meg was asked to color a picture of a duck yellow and orange which she did not do. Moreover, it was sloppy so the teacher threw it in the trash and made Meg redo it. Why could this woman not see what she was doing to my young daughter's spirit? I went home that night and told my husband I was DONE! I could not have my children in a school that broke their wings to fly.

Luckily, that night I attended a parenting group for Indigo children with Karen

Curry and was told about Waldorf schools. The next morning I got on the Internet and found one in my area. Without hesitation, I visited the school and became convinced that this was the place for my children. My husband and I made the decision to register them.

I have never been sorry for making the choices I did. My children are now at a school that honors, loves, and nurtures them the way they need to be. It's amazing to me how different they are now. They don't come home crying, but singing and anxious to tell me about their day.

I was very impressed when Meg's teacher asked me to please buy Meg a pair of rain boots and send in an extra set of clothes. When I questioned her about this, she said, "Because we go on nature walks and I like the children to be able to play in puddles and get as dirty as they want. We then go back to the classroom and need to change clothes." Someone letting my child be a child? The second thing that happened was my nine-year-old, Nate, came home and with great big bright eyes told me,

"Mom, all the children in my class like me and I play with all of them." Now this statement may not sound like much to you, but it was music to my ears for this is a child who was labeled, shunned, ostracized, and made to feel inferior at his old school.

How beautiful it is to be able to watch my children unfold into the wonderful people they are becoming. I had the opportunity to talk to Nate's teacher a few days ago because she was concerned she was not giving him enough. I told her that she is doing the one thing essential for him because ***she loves him***. Without love there is no nurturing and without nurturing there cannot be teaching.

If there is one thing I would want to say to all the parents of special children all over the world, it would be to love them, learn from them, nurture them with understanding, and ***stop medicating them***. Look to the universe for help and guidance.